SCHOLAR Study Guide

Advanced Higher Econo

Authored by:

Colin Spence (Culloden Academy)

Reviewed by:

Wilson Turkington (Edinburgh Academy)

Heriot-Watt University

Edinburgh EH14 4AS, United Kingdom.

First published 2019 by Heriot-Watt University.

This edition published in 2019 by Heriot-Watt University SCHOLAR.

Distributed by the SCHOLAR Forum.

SCHOLAR Study Guide Advanced Higher Economics

Advanced Higher Economics Course Code: C822 77

ISBN 978-1-911057-70-3

Print Production and Fulfilment in UK by Print Trail www.printtrail.com

Acknowledgements

Thanks are due to the members of Heriot-Watt University's SCHOLAR team who planned and created these materials, and to the many colleagues who reviewed the content.

We would like to acknowledge the assistance of the education authorities, colleges, teachers and students who contributed to the SCHOLAR programme and who evaluated these materials.

Grateful acknowledgement is made for permission to use the following material in the SCHOLAR programme:

The Scottish Qualifications Authority for permission to use Past Papers assessments.

The Scottish Government for financial support.

The content of this Study Guide is aligned to the Scottish Qualifications Authority (SQA) curriculum.

Contents

Economic markets

Unit 1 Topic 1

Perfect competition

Contents

Prerequisites

This unit assumes no previous knowledge and is intended to be accessible for those studying Economics for the first time.

However, if you have already completed Higher Economics you will be familiar with some of the concepts.

Learning objective

By the end of this topic you should be able to:

- outline the characteristics of a perfectly competitive market;
- explain the demand and supply curves of a firm in perfect competition;
- explain the short-run positions of super-normal and sub-normal profits;
- explain the long-run equilibrium of the firm.

1.1 What is perfect competition?

Firms face different levels of competition. The markets they operate in are divided by economists into the following categories:

- **monopolistic competition** - describes a market in which firms compete on the basis of differentiating their products from their rivals. This attempt to create a difference, a unique selling proposition, tries to single out the product in the consumers' minds;
- **monopoly** - in theory, refers to a market with only one firm. However, in practical terms, markets where one company dominates can be referred to as monopolies;
- **oligopoly** - refers to a market where a small number of large firms dominate;
- **perfect competition** - has a very large number of firms competing to produce identical products.

Market types Go online 

Q1: Put the following business activities into the correct column for each market type:

- making men's shirts;
- making women's shoes;
- owning all the major UK airports;
- producing "cola" soft drinks;
- producing a patented product;
- producing petrol;
- running all buses in a local area;
- selling computer operating systems;
- selling grade 1 King Edward potatoes;
- selling medium size eggs.

Monopolistic competition	Monopoly	Oligopoly	Perfect competition

All of the markets that are not in perfect competition can be grouped together under the description **imperfect competition**. The term imperfect competition is an umbrella term covering monopolistic competition, monopoly and oligopoly.

In the interests of completeness we will make a brief mention of the term *duopoly*. This describes a form of oligopoly where only two firms dominate a market. Examples might include Coca Cola versus Pepsi Cola in the cola soft drinks market or Unilever versus Proctor and Gamble in the soap powder market.

1.1.1 Requirements for a perfectly competitive market

There are several requirements to be met before a market can be regarded as perfectly competitive:

1. Large number of sellers;
2. Large number of buyers;
3. Homogeneous product;
4. Freedom of entry and exit;
5. Perfect knowledge;
6. Sellers are price takers.

Below are some of the underpinning assumptions of a perfectly competitive market:

- ***Large number of sellers*** - it is essential in perfect competition that the activities of one seller are such a tiny part of the total market that they have negligible impact on the market supply curve. Clearly the decisions of one seller must have some fractional impact on market supply but negligible means that the impact on the market is, to all intents and purposes, imperceptible.

  It follows that the individual output decisions of these sellers cannot shift the supply curve, and they therefore have no influence on the market price.
- ***Large number of buyers*** - no one buyer is large enough to influence the market demand.
- ***Homogeneous product*** - the output of firms in a perfectly competitive market is, to all intents and purposes, identical. Sometimes this requires a narrow definition of the output.

  Eggs would not be sufficiently narrow. However, medium free range eggs might correctly define an identical product in the consumers' eyes. If successfully branded and packaged differently from other medium free range eggs then they are differentiated and no longer homogeneous; the market would no longer be perfect.
- ***Freedom of entry and exit*** - it must be straightforward for firms to come and go from a perfectly competitive market. This requires that there are no large capital requirements, no vast economies of scale, no patents, and that factors of production are perfectly mobile and can switch easily from making one product to making another.
- ***Perfect knowledge*** - information about prices and profits in the market is widely available, and all buyers and sellers can make rational decisions based on this full knowledge.
- ***Sellers are price takers*** - all sellers have to accept the market price because perfect knowledge means that no buyer will offer more.

To summarise, perfect competition is so tightly defined that examples are difficult to find. Typically an agricultural product is used, as there will be thousands of farmers supplying it and a crop variety will conform well to a standard and perhaps be graded. Fields used to produce it can be switched to grow alternative crops and prices are decided by auction in markets.

Perfectly competitive markets Go online 

In each case, select which of the four rules of perfect competition has been broken.

Q2: Pentland Squire-type potatoes are sold in colourful bags and given a brand name.

a) Large number of firms
b) Homogeneous product
c) Freedom of entry and exit
d) Perfect knowledge

b) ....

Q3: Starting up in business mass-producing a cheap car.

a) Large number of firms
b) Homogeneous product
c) Freedom of entry and exit
d) Perfect knowledge

a) ....

Q4: Negotiating discounts with privileged customers.

a) Large number of firms
b) Homogeneous product
c) Freedom of entry and exit
d) Perfect knowledge

d) ....

Q5: Investing in machinery that is use-specific and cannot be adjusted to make other products.

c)

a) Large number of firms
b) Homogeneous product
c) Freedom of entry and exit
d) Perfect knowledge

1.2 The demand curve for a firm in perfect competition

Under conditions of perfect competition, the price is determined by the interaction of supply and demand in the market. When the market has determined the price, the suppliers are unable to exert any influence and must accept the price. The suppliers can be described as **price takers**.

The following illustration shows diagrammatically how price is determined under conditions of perfect competition. The price is the market price for each item sold. Average revenue (AR) is the total revenue divided by the number sold. Marginal revenue (MR) is the price at which the last unit was sold.

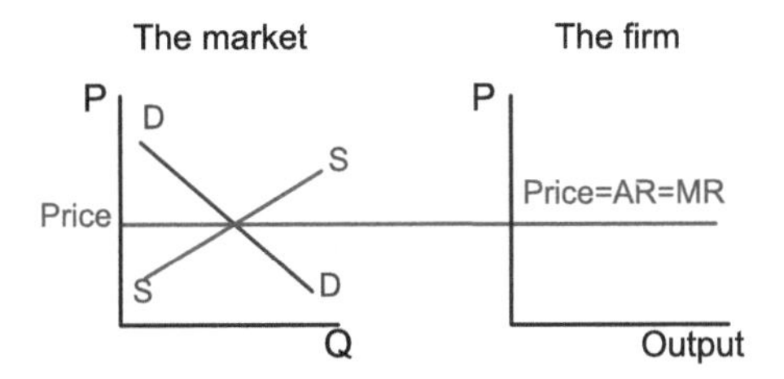

Diagram showing the demand curve for a firm in perfect competition

Under perfect competition, the firm must accept the market price for all units. This means that price = average revenue = marginal revenue.

1.3 The supply curve for a firm in perfect competition

The firm will only produce if it can cover its marginal cost. This is the lowest price at which it would sell one extra unit. Also it will produce nothing in the short-run if it cannot cover its average variable cost (AVC). As a minimum you need to cover wages and material costs, and then make a contribution to paying the firm's fixed costs.

These two rules are illustrated in the following graphs - the line in red is the firm's supply curve.

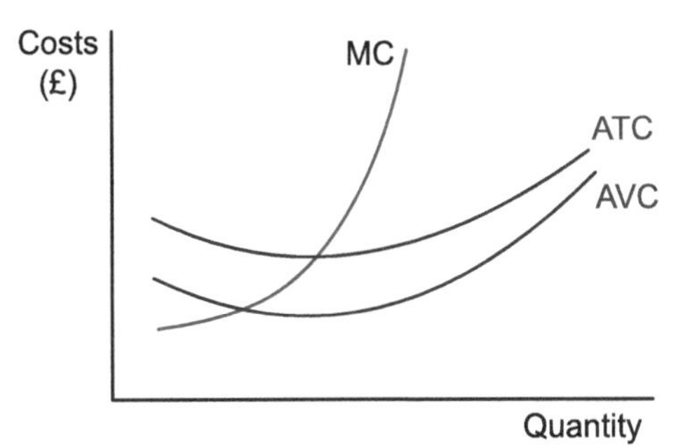

The supply curve under perfect competition

The firm's short-run supply curve is that part of the marginal cost (MC) curve that lies above AVC.

As a previous higher pupil you may remember that:

1. Marginal Cost always cuts Average Total Cost at the lowest point on the ATC curve.
2. The gap between ATC and AVC is Average Fixed Costs, which steadily reduce, hence narrowing the gap as output increases.

1.4 Normal profit

The costs of production are the returns to the four factors of production - wages, rent, interest and profit. So, interestingly, to economists profit is a cost. The costs of production include what is known in economic theory as **normal profit**.

The term "normal profit" is an economic concept that is vital to your understanding of the theory of the firm.

In Economics we assume that entrepreneurs are seeking to make the maximum profit. Consumers, on the other hand, are seeking to maximise their satisfaction (or utility).

Normal profit is a profit that is sufficient to prevent entrepreneurs leaving the industry. It is ***not*** large enough to attract new entrepreneurs into the industry. If an industry gives a below normal profit, entrepreneurs will seek to leave the industry and transfer the resources (factors of production) they control into an industry with above-normal profits.

Under conditions of perfect competition entry and exit from an industry is easy because factors are assumed to be perfectly mobile.

A normal profit is, by definition in Economics, part of the total costs of a firm. In economic theory, when total revenue = total cost (TR = TC), a normal profit is being made. Accountants would differ. They would see this as the break-even point and think of profit as requiring total revenue to exceed total cost. At present you are studying Economics, so set aside the accountants' version, and commit to memory the economic theory.

Normal profit Go online

Q6: The costs of production are the returns to the .... factors of production.

a) four
b) five
c) six

....

Q7: The return to land is ....

a) interest
b) rent
c) profit

....

Q8: The return to capital is ....

a) rent
b) profit
c) interest

....

Q9: The return to labour is ....

a) wages
b) rent
c) profit

....

Q10: The return to enterprise is ....

a) wages
b) interest
c) profit

....

Q11: Economists refer to a profit that neither encourages entry to an industry or exit from an industry as .... profit.

a) gross
b) net
c) normal

1.5 Equilibrium output and marginal cost pricing

In order to make the greatest profit possible, firms must attempt to increase their revenues (money coming into the firm) while decreasing their costs (outgoings). Maximum profits will occur at the output level where total revenue exceeds total costs by the greatest amount. As the profit-maximising firm will be content when the total revenue exceeds total costs by the widest margin, this is called the **equilibrium output**.

Alternatively, profits are maximised at the point where making one more unit (or batch) of output would cost more than the revenue received from selling it. This is the point where marginal cost = marginal revenue (MC = MR). The additional unit (or batch) is termed the marginal unit. Beyond this point the profits will begin to fall back. If the next item costs more to make than it will sell for, then your profits are starting to reduce. The firm will produce where price is equal to marginal cost - this is called **marginal cost pricing**.

1.6 The short-run and perfect competition

The **short-run** in economics is that period during which at least one factor input is fixed.

In the short-run it is possible for a firm in perfect competition to make **super-normal profits**. However because these above normal profits attract entrepreneurs into investing in that industry, they cannot be maintained in the long-run. In the long-run the use of all factors of production can be changed. Hence entrepreneurs will move their factors of production into the super-profit industry, because the factor, enterprise, seeking to maximise profits, directs all factors of production to the most profitable areas.

One of the conditions (or assumptions) of perfect competition is that firms are free to enter and exit the industry. Further, this can happen rapidly due to the assumption that factors of production are perfectly mobile. The graphs below show the how super-profits are competed away by the entry of new firms into the highly profitable industry. In the first set of diagrams, a short-run position with a high price leaves average revenue above average costs - a super-profit for the firm.

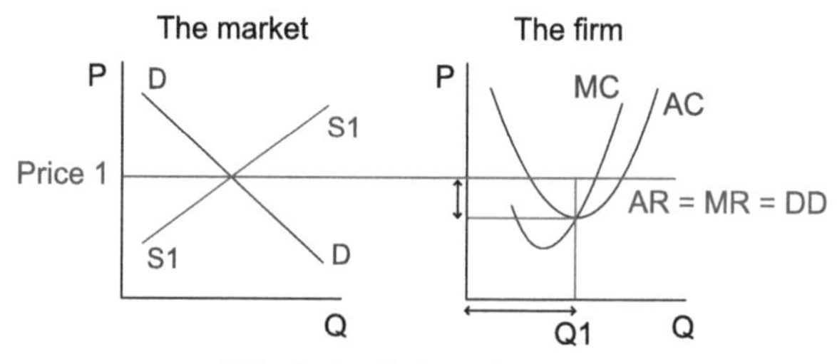

Price before industry investment

New investment into the highly profitable industry takes place. This shifts the market supply curve rightwards to S2 and lowers the market price. Normal profits are then made with AC=AR. Costs in Economics include the returns to all factors of production, including the return of a normal profit to enterprise, so when price (or average revenue) equals average cost then a normal profit is returned.

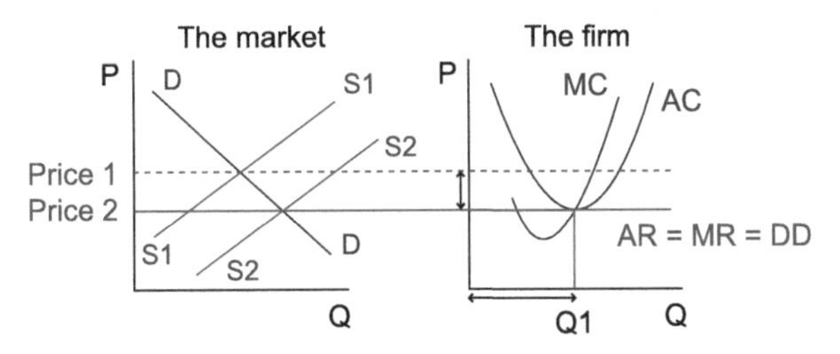

Price after industry investment

In the diagram below, super profits at the output Q1 are the rectangle indicated by the arrows. This is the difference between average revenue and average cost multiplied by the output quantity. Compare the third set of diagrams below to the first set. They are identical, but clarify the extent of the super-profit.

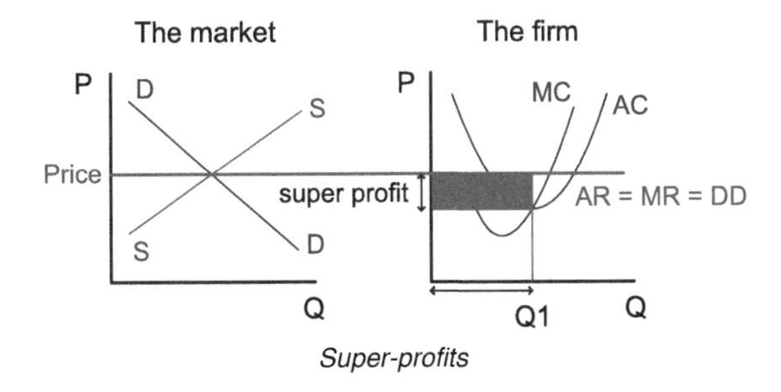

Super-profits

The graphs shows that as new entrants enter the profitable market, supply moves to the right and the market price falls so that for the firm, average revenue equals average cost. This means that the price covers all the costs (rent, wages, interest, and normal profit). Normal profits are within the term "cost" so at this point an economist considers a normal profit is still being made. The firm produces at an output where price equals marginal cost - this is called marginal cost pricing.

You should now be able to work out what will happen when firms in a perfectly competitive market are making **sub-normal profit**. Freedom to exit the industry will result in the supply curve moving to the left. The new intersection of supply and demand will show market price moving upwards. The new higher price will allow those firms left to once again make a normal profit.

Sub-normal profits

Q12: Here are the initial diagrams showing sub-normal profits for the market and the firm. Draw the diagrams for the new position of price after some firms have left this market. Refer to the original graphs for guidance.

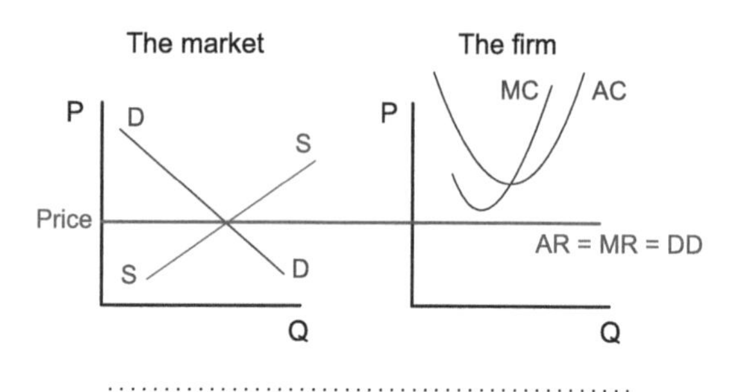

....

Q13: Write a note explaining what has happened in the diagrams.

1.7 Long-run equilibrium

The **long-run** equilibrium of the firm in perfect competition is illustrated in the below.

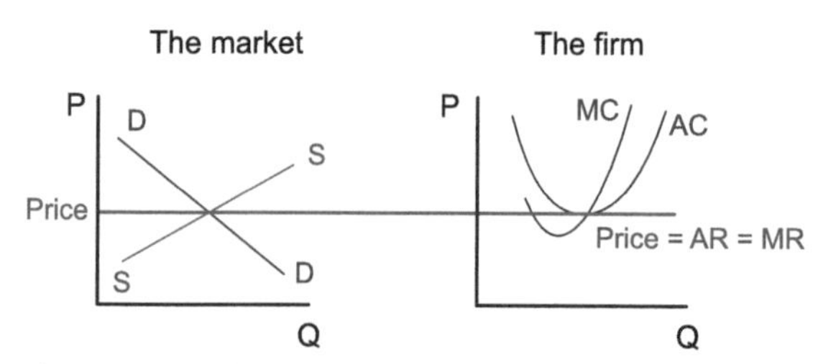

Long-run equilibrium under conditions of perfect competition

The equilibrium price is determined by the interaction of buyers and sellers. They may meet at an auction, or they may trade via computer screen. When the price returned by the market results in normal profits for firms in that industry, then these firms have no inclination to leave the market, nor are new firms attracted. Average cost (including a normal profit) equals average revenue and the market is said to be in long-run equilibrium.

1.8 Summary

Summary

At the end of this topic students should know that:

- perfect competition is a theoretical extreme and the theory of perfect competition helps us to understand the operation of some real world markets. In the real world it is possible to find examples that approximate to perfect competition. The markets for some agricultural products and commodities can be used as examples of near perfect markets;
- the characteristics of a perfect market include: a large number of sellers and a large number of buyers neither of whom have control over the market price of a homogeneous product. They do, however, have perfect knowledge of prices through out the market. Firms face no barriers to entry or exit from the industry;
- the firm's short-run supply curve is that part of the MC curve that lies above average variable cost (AVC);
- the equilibrium of the firm occurs at an output where marginal cost equals marginal revenue. At this point profits are maximised;
- in the short-run, firms in perfect competition may have super-profits or sub-normal profits. Freedom of entry and exit to the industry ensures that in the long-run only normal profits can be made at equilibrium output.

1.9 End of topic test

End of Topic 1 test Go online 

Q14: The following diagram of a short-run perfectly competitive market shows:

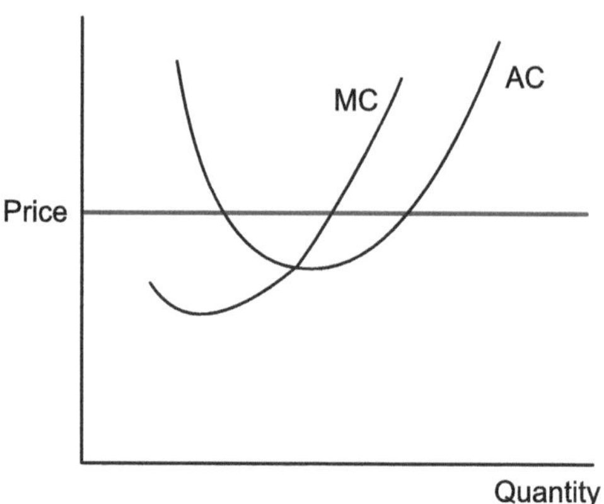

a) normal profits
b) super-normal profits
c) sub-normal profits
d) break-even

....

Q15: Under conditions of perfect competition, in long-run equilibrium:

a) normal profits can be made.
b) firms will enter the industry to obtain super-profits.
c) resources will be switched to the manufacture of other products.
d) price will exceed marginal cost.

....

Q16: Which of the following is **not** a characteristic of a perfectly competitive market?

a) Perfect knowledge of the market.
b) Freedom of entry and exit from the market.
c) Large economies of scale.
d) Many sellers.

....

Q17: The term 'normal profit':

a) refers to average revenue exceeding average cost.
b) refers to a profit that is above the costs of production.
c) is one cost within the costs of production.
d) is insufficient to keep companies in an industry.

....

Q18: In perfect competition a firm will stop producing in the short-run if price is less than:

a) average total cost.
b) marginal cost.
c) average variable cost.
d) average fixed cost.

Unit 1 Topic 2

Advantages and disadvantages of perfect competition

Contents

Learning objective

By the end of this topic you should be able to:

- outline the conditions required for perfect competition;
- explain the advantages of perfect competition;
- explain the disadvantages of perfect competition;
- describe examples of near perfect competition.

2.1 The conditions for perfect competition

Generally in Economics it is assumed that firms act to maximise their profits whereas consumers act to maximise their satisfaction (or utility). It is assumed that the behaviour of firms is such that they seek to make the greatest profit possible, i.e. firms will maximise profit and are not considered likely to sell at lower prices than they could get away with. Also built into this assumption is the expectation that firms will do everything possible to minimise costs.

The conditions for perfect competition include the following:

- ***Equilibrium price*** - In a perfect market, the price is decided by the forces of supply and demand interacting in the market, creating a market clearing or **equilibrium price**. At this price there is no excess supply and all that is available at the price is taken up by demand. Any surplus leads to cuts in price until the price is sufficiently low to sell everything. Equally there is no excess demand because the equilibrium price is just enough to put off some purchasers who choose to gain more utility from a different purchase in a different market.

  When the price mechanism settles at an equilibrium it will still be buffeted by fresh alterations in supply and demand but whatever the price is on a given day is the price that must be taken by the sellers. The selling firms seek to maximise profits so will not be taking a lower price than the market price. The selling firms, operating in conditions of perfect competition, are supplying to a market where the buyers have perfect knowledge of the prices charged by all of their competitors.

- ***Firms are price takers*** - Further, given that the product is unbranded and entirely identical to its rivals' products, why would buyers choose to pay more than the prevailing market price? A combination of perfect knowledge and a homogeneous product forces the firm to accept the market price as the best on offer at any given moment. **Firms operating in perfectly competitive markets are therefore described as price takers.** They can choose what level of production to bring to market but, because they represent a negligible part of total market supply, their output decision cannot affect equilibrium price.

- ***Normal profits (freedom of entry and exit to the industry)*** - In the long-run under perfect competition, super-profits cannot be made by firms. If super-profits existed in the short run they would be competed away as new entrants joined the industry. It is a condition of perfect competition that entrepreneurs face no difficulties in moving their resources into and out of these markets. For example there cannot be high capital costs to join a perfectly competitive industry as that would offend the principle of easy entry.

- ***Large numbers of buyers and sellers*** - The requirement of a large numbers of sellers makes **collusion** between sellers most unlikely to succeed. Again, consumers are likely to get a "square deal" in a perfectly competitive market. Consumers are also not allowed to corrupt the perfect market by being major players or grouping together on the buying side of the market. This is best ensured by the condition that there should be large numbers of buyers and sellers.

- ***Homogeneous products*** - Products in perfect competition must be **homogeneous**. The product made by one firm must be graded as identical to the products sold by all the other firms in that market. No branding or marketing or packaging is allowed as this leaves it open for imagined differences to occur in consumers' minds and good sales people and marketing managers will quickly exploit these product differences.
- ***Perfect knowledge*** - In these days of the mobile phone and the internet, **perfect knowledge** no longer seems such a difficult condition to meet. It is assumed that all buyers and sellers are aware of prices everywhere else in the market for a product. There is no hiding place for those who would seek to set a price different from the market price.

The conditions for perfect competition

Q1: Decide which of the following are conditions for perfect competition are true or false and put them into the correct column:

- Few firms;
- Identical products;
- Local monopoly;
- Many buyers;
- Many sellers;
- Normal profits;
- Perfect knowledge;
- Price leaders;
- Price makers;
- Price takers;
- Product differentiation;
- Profit maximising.

True	False

2.2 The advantages of perfect competition

The advantages of perfect competition include:

- marginal cost pricing;
- low prices and no consumer exploitation.

The greatest advantage of perfect competition is that consumers pay a low price that equals marginal cost. This is termed ***marginal cost pricing***.

The price of the purchase equals exactly the cost of the resources used to produce it. These resources had alternative uses so their cost represents the opportunity cost of foregone production of other goods. It has become impossible to produce more of the purchased good without increasing marginal cost (or opportunity cost). The price that the purchaser is willing to pay is exactly equal to the cost to the company of producing the good. Company costs include a normal profit. This is the point of **economic efficiency**. Any further increase in production of the good will lower the value of output of the economy as the resources cannot be used in a more economically efficient way.

Refer to the previous section ***1.6 The short-run and perfect competition*** to revise the explanation of how a perfectly competitive market arrives at a long-run equilibrium with normal profit.

Low prices and no consumer exploitation are therefore reputed to be an advantage of markets that are in perfect (or near perfect) competition. Companies that try to charge a higher price lose customers to rivals. Customers are aware of the prices available in the market (perfect knowledge) and will go elsewhere for an identical (homogeneous) product.

2.3 The disadvantages of perfect competition

There are several possible disadvantages of a market composed of many fairly small firms:

- ***Few economies of scale*** - Freedom of entry means that the capital cost of setting up in that industry is low. This implies that there are no significant economies of scale. Prices to consumers might be lower if firms were sizeable enough to enjoy economies of scale. Economies of scale create greater efficiencies, cutting costs and prices to consumers.
- ***Natural monopolies*** - Some industries are not suited to perfect competition. They may be natural monopolies. It would make little sense having many small gas companies compete if they all used their own pipes. Imagine the costs and the frequency with which the roads would be dug up.

  Under these circumstances only one body should be responsible for the pipes in any area; it will have a monopoly on the gas pipes. Otherwise costs and hence prices to consumers will be higher. Some industries are inefficient and wasteful if operated by a multitude of small firms.
- ***Funds for research and development*** - Normal profits are unlikely to be enough to finance much research into new products. Firms are unlikely to take great risks by researching new

products many of which will never get to market unless they expect to receive profits that are commensurate with the risks. Thus, perfect competition may not lead to high levels of innovation. This makes them statically efficient - there is no incentive to research to become dynamically more efficient over time.

Natural monopoly Go online 

Q2: Which of the following could be considered a natural monopoly in the UK:

a) Railway tracks and electricity power lines
b) Railway tracks and water pipes
c) Electricity power lines and water pipes
d) Railway tracks, electricity power lines and water pipes

Advantages and disadvantages of perfect competition Go online

Q3: Collusion unlikely.

a) Advantage
b) Disadvantage

....

Q4: Economically efficient market structure.

a) Advantage
b) Disadvantage

....

Q5: Few economies of scale.

a) Advantage
b) Disadvantage

....

Q6: Limited research.

a) Advantage
b) Disadvantage

....

Q7: Low prices.

a) Advantage
b) Disadvantage

2.4 An example of near perfect competition

A perfect example of perfect competition does not exist. The theory of perfect competition is just that - a theory. It is an extreme position that can only fully exist as a theoretical concept. However, it guides us in our understanding of markets that display many of its conditions. Several markets approximate to perfect competition.

The price of fish

'Mackerel and red mullet' (http://bit.ly/1B6ZQdy) by Jeremy Keith (http://bit.ly/1FdD7vS) is licensed under CC BY 2.0 (http://bit.ly/17p9WuW)

The price of fish in this market illustrates several components of the theory of perfect competition.

1. The supply of fish comes from many boats acting independently. There are many more boats landing fish at other harbours up and down the country.
2. The demand for fish comes from many buyers (fishmongers, fish processing plants, restaurants). They are in competition for the fish that have been landed. The buyers are professional and knowledgeable about their market.
3. An auction takes place to establish a market clearing price. Fish do not keep well, so it is important that the market is cleared that morning. The interaction of buyers and sellers decides the price of fish. If you want to sell your fish you will have to accept the prevailing price set by the market. Sellers are price takers.
4. Buyers can be in contact with other ports by mobile phone so can be aware of prices elsewhere - perhaps approximating to perfect knowledge.
5. The sellers may be able to land fish at a choice of ports depending on the prices they expect to meet - modern communications and market knowledge.
6. The boat owners want to maximise their profits.

The skills and courage of the fishermen are in limited supply and the fishing boats filled with the latest technology are extremely expensive. Therefore freedom of entry into this industry is not fulfilled. The "sunk costs" (no pun intended) that are incurred when a boat is purchased may also make leaving the industry difficult. A fishing boat is not a piece of capital that readily adapts to life in a different line of work!

The market is also subject to restrictions and catch quotas to prevent over-fishing. Here we have an example of government intervention in a market - a topic we return to later.

Fishing industry Go online

Q8: Perfect knowledge in the fishing industry has been enhanced by the use of mobile phones by buyers.

a) True
b) False

....

Q9: Fishermen have to accept the market price on the quayside.

a) True
b) False

....

Q10: Boat owners can collude to arrange higher prices.

a) True
b) False

....

Q11: The fishing industry is not an example of perfect competition because:

a) capital used cannot easily adapt to other uses.
b) there are few buyers of fish.
c) fish are in increasingly short supply.
d) buyers are not in contact with other fishing ports.

....

Q12: Perfect competition requires that entry and exit from an industry are easy. It is easy for an entrepreneur to:

a) enter the fishing industry.
b) exit the fishing industry.
c) neither enter nor exit the fishing industry.
d) both enter and exit the fishing industry.

Other markets in near perfect competition Go online 

Q13: Carry out some research on the internet into how the market for either:

a) a currency or
b) an agricultural crop;

resembles perfect competition. Present your answer in the style of the section on the price of fish above. That is, summarise your conclusions in a numbered list as above.

2.5 Summary

Summary

At the end of this topic students should know that:

- The conditions required for perfect competition are:
  - profit maximising behaviour by firms;
  - a large number of buyers and sellers;
  - an homogeneous product;
  - perfect knowledge;
  - freedom of entry and exit;
  - firms are price takers;
- The advantages of perfect competition are:
  - prices equal to marginal cost making it (theoretically) an economically efficient market structure;
  - firms are unable to exploit consumers and maintain super-profits in the long-run;
- The disadvantages of perfect competition are:
  - few economies of scale can be attained;
  - funds for researching new products are limited.

2.6 End of topic test

End of Topic 2 test Go online

Q14: Which of the following are advantages of perfect competition?

a) A standardised product
b) Price is equal to marginal price
c) Both of the above
d) Neither of the above

....

Q15: One disadvantage of perfect competition is:

a) low prices.
b) super profits.
c) economic efficiency.
d) fewer economies of scale.

....

Q16: Under perfect competition prices are:

a) the cost of labour and capital.
b) the cost of labour, capital and rent.
c) the cost of labour, capital, rent and a normal profit.
d) the cost of labour, capital, rent and a super-normal profit.

....

Q17: Which of the following is a characteristic of perfect competition?

a) Low prices
b) Super profits
c) Large economies of scale
d) High capital costs

....

Q18: The market for a product such as crisps cannot be perfect due to:

a) branded products.
b) differentiated products.
c) both of the above.
d) neither of the above.

....

Q19: Which of the following correctly shows a gain and a loss for consumers in a perfect market?

a) Low prices due to economies of scale but a standardised product.
b) High levels of research and development but consumers are exploited.
c) Product differentiation but limited economies of scale prevent still lower prices.
d) Competition reduces prices but limited funds for research.

....

Q20: Outline the main differences between the concept of perfect competition and the market circumstances that a small suburban grocer's shop faces. *(10 marks)*

Hints:

- Are food sales in the UK dominated by a few large firms?
- How does your location affect the conditions of perfect competition?
- Will you sell everything at the same price as other shops?
- Can the competition just set up across the road?
- Do customers know the price of everything, everywhere?

Unit 1 Topic 3

Monopoly

Contents

Learning objective

By the end of this topic you should be able to:

- define monopoly;
- explain how barriers to entry work to maintain monopoly;
- explain the profit maximising position of a monopolist;
- explain the disadvantages of monopoly for society;
- outline the benefits of monopoly.

3.1 Defining monopoly

A monopoly is a market that has only one supplier. There are no close substitutes for the monopolist's output. This means that the downward sloping demand curve for the entire market is, in the absence of any competitors, the demand curve faced by the monopolist.

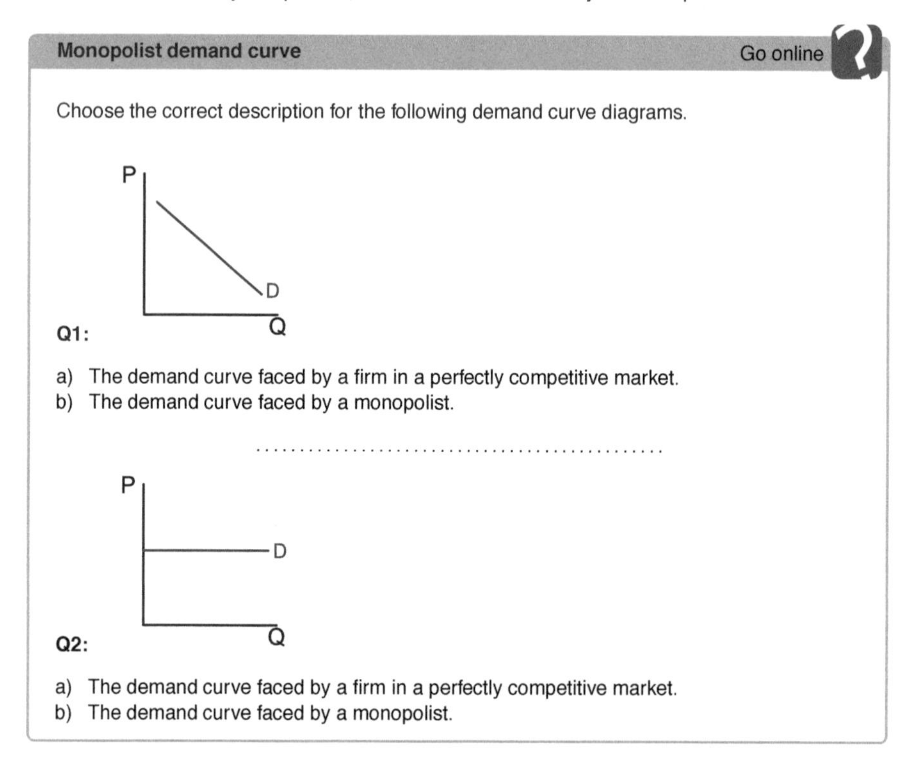

Monopolist demand curve Go online

Choose the correct description for the following demand curve diagrams.

Q1:

a) The demand curve faced by a firm in a perfectly competitive market.
b) The demand curve faced by a monopolist.

....

Q2:

a) The demand curve faced by a firm in a perfectly competitive market.
b) The demand curve faced by a monopolist.

In contrast to the horizontal demand curve faced by a firm in perfect competition, the monopolist's demand curve is therefore downward sloping left to right - just like a normal demand curve. This gives the monopolist control over either price or output. If the monopolist sets a price, the consumers make the decision whether to buy or not at that price. If the monopolist were to select an output level, then the market through the demand curve will decide on the price they can charge to sell it all.

The market demand curve is the same as the monopolist's average revenue (selling price) at each output level.

That is the theory. Meanwhile, in the real world, it can be very difficult to define a market in a way that does not overlap into a neighbouring market. If one company had a monopoly of railways that would only be a completely effective monopoly if the railway industry did not overflow into the wider transport industry. As potential customers may choose private cars, buses, and aeroplanes as alternatives, having a rail monopoly is not all it seems.

Defining monopoly Go online

Q3: In a monopoly market there is only one supplier.

a) True
b) False

....

Q4: A monopoly faces a horizontal demand curve.

a) True
b) False

....

Q5: A monopoly controls the price and the demand.

a) True
b) False

....

Q6: Consumers have no close substitutes for the monopoly's product.

a) True
b) False

3.2 Barriers to entry

Barriers to entry make it difficult for new firms to move into the same market as an established monopoly. These are advantages that the established monopolist has that the new entrant does not have. According to the economist Joseph Stiglitz barriers to entry are "a cost of producing which must be borne by a firm which seeks to enter an industry but is not borne by firms already in the industry".

Some examples of typical barriers to entry are:

- ***Patents*** - A patent grants a legal right to the owners of the patent (not always the inventor) to have a monopoly on making, using or selling a patented product for a fixed period of time. Trade marks and copyright restrictions are similar. It is up to the owner of the patent to safeguard the patent through legal action taken against those who infringe it. This can be expensive.
- ***Licences and franchises*** - A licence to operate gives official permission to companies or individuals. Licences can be granted by government. The UK Government has granted regional franchises to both television channels and railway companies for the payment of a fee to the government. These licences are usually offered to the highest bidder (in some cases the bid requiring the lowest subsidy wins) and stop other firms from entering these markets for the duration of the licence.

- ***Economies of scale*** - An established firm may already be operating on a large scale and benefiting from low average costs. For example it may be buying materials in bulk and receiving substantial discounts from suppliers. Mass production will also ensure that the established firm receives technical economies. New firms trying to gain a foothold in the market are unable to match the low production costs and hence low customer prices of the established firm.
- ***Startup costs*** - Entering the market may require a vast initial capital cost. The plant purchased may not be adaptable to other uses so that leaving the industry in failure may involve writing off large sums of money. The "sunk costs" may not be recoverable. Thus startup costs act as a disincentive to new firms. However, if the potential returns are commensurate with the level of risk, it should be possible to find capital in the market place for the project.
- ***Existing brand loyalty*** - The established firm will be recognised by consumers who will routinely pick that familiar brand. These habits will be reinforced by advertising. Breaking into these patterns of behaviour would prove expensive, requiring low launch prices and costly advertising.
- ***Predatory pricing*** - The established firm may temporarily depart from its profit-maximising prices to stamp on a new entrant. For example, a major bus company with a regional monopoly may undercut the fares of a new entrant or run more buses on a route just to force the new entrant into early bankruptcy. Once the monopoly has been re-established the bus fares move rapidly back to their original high levels or higher.
- ***Vertical integration*** (control over raw materials, components, and market outlets) - Companies that combine through merger or takeover to create vertically integrated operations can make it difficult for new firms to acquire raw materials or components. Alternatively they may own the most obvious market outlet for the new competitor and thus prevent it acquiring sufficient shelf space in front of the consumer. It is possible to design contracts with suppliers or retailers that similarly interfere with competition without actually acquiring these suppliers or retailers as subsidiaries.

Barriers to entry Go online 

Q7: Match the following descriptions to the terms in the table below and put them in the correct row:

- Heinz Baked Beans in the shopping trolley every week;
- How Dyson stopped Hoover copying (for a while);
- Low prices used to bankrupt competitor;
- Mass producing low cost cars;
- Required to run a municipal taxi;
- Surveying, drilling, refining and retailing oil.

Terms	Descriptions
Licence	
Brand loyalty	
Vertical integration	
Patents	
Predatory pricing	
Economies of scale	

3.3 Profit maximisation

Profit maximisation for a monopoly is illustrated on the following diagram:

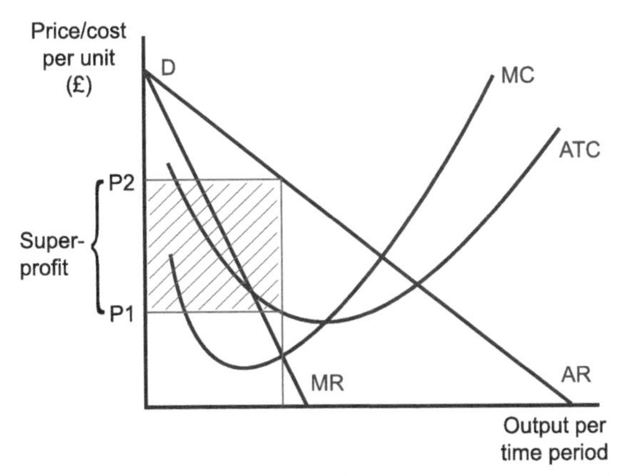

Profit maximisation diagram comparing cost per unit against output

The diagram can be best understood one line (straight and curved) at a time:

- The demand line (D) represents the possible price and output combinations of the monopolist. When a monopolist sets the price, the consumers through the market demand curve decide how much they will purchase. As there are no other suppliers of the product, the market demand line is the average revenue line of the monopolist. This is the line on the diagram labelled D at one end and AR at the other end.
- The marginal revenue line (MR) falls at twice the slope (or at half the angle if you prefer) of the average revenue line.

- The U-shaped average total cost curve (ATC) is cut, as always, at its lowest point by the marginal cost curve (MC).

Profit-maximising point

The profit-maximising point occurs where producing one more unit of output (the marginal unit) would give marginal revenue equal to the marginal cost of making it. Beyond this, the cost of making another unit would exceed the revenue returned - and therefore profits would begin to reduce.

Therefore the vertical line at output quantity Q, which runs through the intersection of MR and MC, is the key to the profit maximising of the monopolist. Continue this line upwards through the average total cost curve until it hits the average revenue (or market demand) line.

Super-profit

The lower red-coloured line leading to the vertical axis marks the average cost and the upper line marks the average revenue. The difference between them is the super-profit made by the monopolist per unit sold. Remember that a normal profit is included in the term average cost, and anything above average cost is an above normal or super-profit.

Finally notice the rectangle that the upper and lower orange lines are top and bottom boundaries to. This multiplies the super-profit per unit by the units of output to give a diagrammatic representation of super-profits at the profit maximising output level of Q.

If there are barriers to entry these super-profits can be maintained in the long-run because no competitors will enter the market and compete prices and profits downwards. Therefore, we have now established the short-run and long-run equilibrium of a profit maximising monopolist.

Build your own profit maximisation diagram

On paper build up your own profit maximisation diagram.

1. Label the axes correctly.
2. Draw the two diagonal lines AR and MR, remembering that the slope of MR is twice as great.
3. Draw a U-shaped ATC curve that sweeps down and then upwards.
4. Carefully add in the MC curve which must cut ATC at its lowest point.
5. Next draw up a vertical line from the horizontal axis through the MC=MR intersection and on to the AR line.
6. Finally add in the two horizontal lines that go out to the ATC and AR lines to meet your vertical line.

7. You could now shade in the rectangle of super-profit.

Once completed, carefully compare your drawing with the diagram above.

Monopolist's cost and revenue table Go online 

Q8: Complete the following cost and revenue table for a monopolist.

Output units	Price (AR) per unit	TR (£)	TC (£)	Profit (£)	MC (£)	MR (£)	ATC (£)
0	100		50		n/a	n/a	n/a
1	80		90				
2	75		120				
3	70		144				
4	65		160				
5	60		180				
6	55		210				
7	50		259				
8	45		312				
9	40		369				
10	35		440				

Cost and revenue diagram for a monopolist 

Q9: Use the figures in the above answer to construct a diagram showing the profit maximising price and output of this monopolist.

3.4 The disadvantages of monopoly

The disadvantages of monopoly include the following:

- ***Efficiency loss*** - Economic efficiency requires that the prices faced by consumers reflect the true cost of the factors of production involved in the production process (price equal to marginal cost). If consumers are overcharged for a product then the opportunity cost of that product has increased and the good is likely to be under-consumed. This is economically less efficient. The true cost of production would leave the factor, i.e. enterprise, with a normal profit and not an above-normal profit.
- ***Lack of choice for consumers*** - With only one producer of a product in the market place the consumers face a lack of options. They may buy the product at the price or not buy it but there are no substitutes available.

- ***Higher prices*** - Prices can be maintained above marginal cost in the long-run. The lack of any competition enables the monopolist to charge higher prices and make above-normal profits.
- ***Less innovation*** - In the absence of competitive pressure, companies may be in no rush to introduce new products or invest in research and development. With the old "cash cow" still selling so well and being so profitable, and having sunk costs in the old capital equipment, companies might extend its lifetime.

Disadvantages of a monopoly Go online 

Q10: Decide which of the following are disadvantages of monopoly and put them into the table below:

- Economically inefficient
- Economies of scale
- Higher prices
- Low prices
- Many sellers
- No choice
- Normal profits
- Predatory pricing
- Price = marginal cost
- Slow innovation

Disadvantages of a monopoly

3.5 The benefits of monopoly

The benefits of monopoly include the following:

- ***Economies of scale*** - Consumers may receive lower prices as a result of the economies of scale gained by a monopolist. It is feasible that gains to consumers arising from the reduction in prices due to economies of scale may be greater than the losses to consumers caused by the absence of competition in the market. Monopolists are anxious not to draw attention to their dominant position as this may lead to political intervention to curtail it. Typically, therefore, a monopolist does not charge the maximum price they could.
- ***Innovation, research and development*** - It can be argued that monopoly super-profit enables a firm to take a long-term view of investment, assured that its strategic plans will

not be buffeted by short-term competitive pressures. Budgets for research and development are maintained through profits and the consumer gains from new products. For example, drug companies would claim that patents for new medicines allow them to take this approach with the initial high profits from newly patented drugs.

- ***Natural monopolies*** - Some industries are not suited to perfect competition and are too inefficient and wasteful if operated by a multitude of small firms. This is the case for **natural monopolies** where allowing competition would lead to higher costs that would be passed on as higher prices. Under these circumstances only one body should be responsible for the infrastructure, otherwise each separate set of capital would be under-used. For example, it would make little sense having competing railway companies if they all used their own infrastructure with each separate railway paying separate costs including maintenance, building of rails, stations, bridges and tunnels.

The benefits of monopoly Go online

Q11: Monopolies can lead to cheaper products because of the economies of scale achieved.

a) True
b) False

....

Q12: Natural monopolies would face higher costs if split into competitive firms.

a) True
b) False

....

Q13: Monopolies are under pressure to innovate.

a) True
b) False

....

Q14: Monopolies may use super-profits to fund long-term research.

a) True
b) False

3.6 Summary

Summary

At the end of this topic students should know that:

- in theory, a monopolist is the only supplier of a product for which there is no close substitute;
- barriers to entry are required to maintain the monopoly and prevent other firms from setting up to make the same product;
- monopolists can maintain super-profit in the long-run because barriers to entry exclude rivals;
- a monopolist faces a downward sloping demand curve which is the demand curve for the entire market;
- if a monopolist charges the price where marginal revenue equals marginal cost, then the gap between average revenue and average cost at this price, multiplied by the output, equals the maximum super-profit realised by the monopolist;
- a natural monopoly exists when the only efficient way to organise an industry is to have only one firm;
- a monopoly is generally associated with costs such as higher prices and economic inefficiency but it also conveys benefits such as vast economies of scale that can cut costs and prices;
- many monopolists keep a low profile and avoid political intervention by charging less than the profit maximising price.

3.7 End of topic test

End of Topic 3 test Go online 

Q15: Which of the following are generally true of a monopoly and could benefit the consumer over the long term?

a) Economies of scale
b) Standardised products
c) High levels of innovation
d) Predatory pricing

....

Q16: The profits made by a monopolist are maximised where:

a) Price = Marginal Cost
b) Average Cost = Average Revenue
c) Marginal Cost = Marginal Revenue
d) Average Cost = Marginal Revenue

....

Q17: Monopolies make:

a) short-run super-profits.
b) long-run super-profits.
c) both short-run and long-run super-profits.
d) neither short-run nor long-run super-profits.

....

Q18: Barriers to entry into a monopoly market include:

a) economies of scale and high prices.
b) economies of scale and vertical integration.
c) high prices and vertical integration.
d) economies of scale, high prices and vertical integration.

....

Q19: Which of the following describes two characteristics of a monopoly?

a) Prices are lower and the consumer faces limited choice.
b) Prices are higher and new firms can enter the market.
c) Prices are lower and the firm can protect super-profits in the long run.
d) Prices are higher and barriers prevent new entrants to the market.

Q20: Compare and contrast monopoly with perfect competition. *(10 marks)*

Hint: Compare the number and size of sellers, the influence over price, profitability in the short-run and long-run, the economic efficiency, and the level of barriers to entry.

Unit 1 Topic 4

Monopolistic competition

Contents

Learning objective

By the end of this topic students should be able to:

- define monopolistic competition;
- explain the characteristics of a monopolistic competition;
- explain the profit maximising position of a firm in monopolistic competition in both the short and long run;
- describe examples of markets that illustrate monopolistic competition.

4.1 Defining monopolistic competition

Monopolistic competition describes a common market structure that involves many firms producing differentiated (not homogeneous) products that compete with each other for consumers' attention. It is a world of variety and close substitutes where design features and marketing are as important as price.

The theory of monopolistic competition was developed in the 1930s when economists needed a model that was closer to the real world in which companies operated. They came to regard the extreme models of perfect competition and monopoly as inadequate on their own as an explanation of market structures. Firms did not attain these theoretical positions.

If there is so much competition going on where does the term "monopolistic" come from? In a sense as the products are not identical, each firm is seeking to create differences that render its product unique. This is what a business student may term a USP (unique selling proposition). The product seeks to be unique in the mind of the consumer and different from its competitors - to create in effect its own monopoly position as a sole supplier in some way special and different from all the close alternatives.

The diagrams below show the short and long-tun equilibrium positions of a profit-maximising monopolistic competitor.

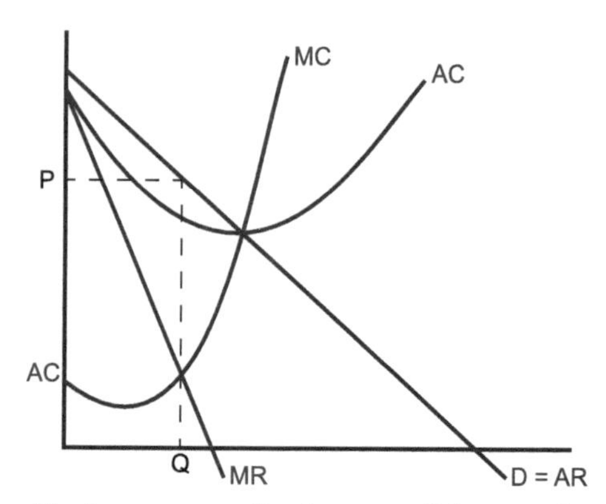

Short-run super-profits of a monopolistic competitor

In the short-run a super-profit is possible. The small gap between AR and AC results in above normal profits. Remember that a normal profit to the factor of production, enterprise, is included in average cost, so revenue beyond this is a super-profit.

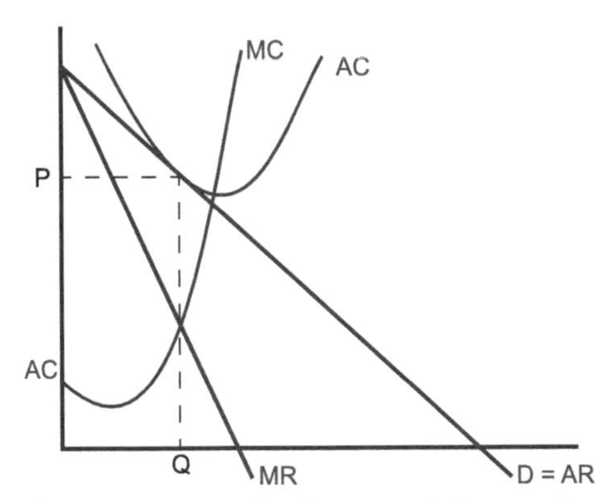

Long-run super-profits of a monopolistic competitor

In the long-run (unlike in a monopoly) the entry of new firms to the super-profitable market cannot be prevented. In the long-run, super-profits are competed away and normal profits resume. Therefore average revenue will only cover average cost.

Monopolistic competition background reading Go online 

Use a search engine for "monopolistic competition" and find some background reading on the internet. You may also wish to refer to Tutor2u (https://www.tutor2u.net/) or Economics Help (http://bit.ly/1PJN7X5) .

Make notes from your reading on a word document. Consider printing these out for your folder. Alternatively you may wish to save your findings on computer or to memory stick.

Monopolistic competition video Go online 

A YouTube video on monopolistic competition (https://youtu.be/T3F1Vt3lyNc) may help your understanding.

4.2 Characteristics of monopolistic competition

The following are typical features of a market in monopolistic competition:

- there are many firms (but not as many as in perfect competition);
- each firm has a small share of the total market for that type of product;
- there is an effort to **differentiate** your product from other similar products of the same type;
- there is some control over price because your product is unique or distinctive in some way;

- marketing and **branding** are used to create distinct identities in the market place - the differences in your product can be real and tangible or placed in consumers' imagination by the adoption of a certain style of marketing.

The following features tend not to be present in monopolistic competition, so their absence may indicate such a market:

- reacting to or second-guessing the behaviour of other firms (game theory) is difficult because of the large number of other firms;
- firms do not cooperate or collude with each other as fixing prices in the market would be very difficult because of the large number of selling firms.

Characteristics of monopolistic competition Go online

Q1: Monopolistic competition describes a market in which one firm is dominant.

a) True
b) False

....

Q2: In monopolistic competition products are not identical.

a) True
b) False

....

Q3: Prices are set by the market and the firms operating in monopolistic competition has no influence.

a) True
b) False

....

Q4: Collusion among firms is commonplace under monopolistic competition.

a) True
b) False

....

Q5: In monopolistic competition each firm creates a unique brand in the market.

a) True
b) False

4.3 Examples of monopolistic competition

The vast majority of firms operate in conditions of monopolistic competition. Supermarket products and clothing retailers' stocks come from firms operating within this market structure. (Ironically, in the UK the supermarkets themselves are an example of oligopoly.)

The brand name is almost always significant to the consumer, who will identify or not identify with the brand image and reputation. Brands are valuable assets and hard-headed business executives spend small fortunes advertising brands to prove it.

One way of identifying this type of market structure is to look at the concentration ratio. Within a local area, for example, there may be only a few firms operating. Consider the market share of the largest four or five firms in the industry, and if this gives a low percentage then the industry is usually in monopolistic competition. A high percentage would indicate an oligopoly which is domination by a few large firms.

Examples of monopolistic competition include:

- ***The restaurant trade*** - There may be only six restaurants in a small town. However the ease with which newcomers can enter the industry and set up in competition would make this typical of monopolistic competition. Product differentiation will occur through differences in menu, ambience, location and opening hours. This is also typical of monopolistic competition.
- ***The hairdressing trade*** - A local hairdresser is offering the same type of service as other local hairdressers but not exactly the same service. The hairdresser will have a particular level of skill but not an identical level of skill. The decoration and appearance of the salon will be different as will its location and the facilities for parking. Even the conversation of the hairdresser with the customer will differ as will the general manner of the staff. These subtle differences are the stuff of monopolistic competition.
- ***The clothing trade*** - Most areas of the clothing and fashion trade exhibit the characteristics of monopolistic competition.

4.4 Product differentiation

Of all the characteristics of monopolistic competition, **product differentiation** is the most significant. For example, if Tesco brand a packet of oranges as "finest" - one of their own label brands - then consumers expect a quality difference compared to the "value" brand. They may be willing to pay more for this, and they may indeed taste better.

The nature of the packaging may even be part of the added value of the product. Fruit and vegetables, for example, can be packaged instead of being sold loose.

Not all differences are tangible. Some images associated with the product through successful advertising campaigns are placed in the consumers' minds. Products are marketed to appeal to particular market segments. For many consumers the ultimate orange may not be just any orange, but a Marks and Spencer's orange, as this company has spent heavily to brand their food at the quality end of the market.

When you next pass the oranges have a look at the bananas! One well-known retailer used to pile them high into trays, whereas another one hung them carefully on hooks. Here we have a product that may have initially been priced for the grower under conditions approaching perfect competition, being sold in an oligopolistic UK supermarket, in a differentiated (monopolistic competition) way.

Product differentiation in the footwear industry

Q6: Most areas of the clothing and fashion trade exhibit the characteristics of monopolistic competition and product differentiation.

Make a list of the number of ways in which footwear can be differentiated. Give yourself a target of ten ways of differentiation.

Product differentiation for oranges

Visit the stores for three different supermarket chains (e.g. Morrisons, Marks & Spencer, Lidl) or check online.

Have a look at the different varieties, prices and packaging for oranges. As an agricultural crop, you may have thought of oranges as an example of "perfect competition" but by the time they hit the shelves they are differentiated in several ways. Make a list of the ways in which oranges are differentiated.

Product differentiation summary

Q7: Complete the paragraph below by filling in the spaces with the missing words.

Product .... is a feature of monopolistic competition. A firm will create a .... with its own unique .... However, many close .... will be available to consumers. Expenditure on .... assists in creating consumer brand loyalty. This allows the firm some influence over .... It makes the brand less price ....

4.5 Advertising in monopolistic competition

Products in monopolistically competitive markets have many close substitutes competing for attention and all different to some extent. Advertising budgets are substantial as, while price is an important aspect of the marketing mix, promotional activity is equally significant for these products. They have, after all, to get their difference across.

If they succeed, they should benefit from lower price elasticity of demand. If more consumers view their product as in some way different or unique, then the substitutes will not be as close as they were. Closeness of substitutes affects price elasticity of demand and having differentiated from them successfully, your customers will be less prone to leave you in response to price changes.

Advertising can increase market share and the increased sales can lead to greater economies of scale cutting production costs. Advertising can even increase the whole size of the market. This happened during one of Levi Strauss & Co's successful jeans campaigns. Sales of Levi's rocketed and sales of all other brands of jeans went up as well.

Advertising budgets Go online 

Go on to the internet and carry out some research on advertising budgets.

Search using the words "top UK advertisers". It should be possible to find several examples of large advertising budgets. Be careful as some examples will be for companies in oligopolistic markets as well as for those in monopolistic competition.

Advertising in monopolistic competition Go online 

Q8: Decide which of the following statements describe advantages and disadvantages of advertising and put them into the correct column in the table below:

- Adds to the cost of products;
- Can be visual pollution;
- Can mislead and fail to deliver the promised utility to buyers;
- Creates jobs;
- Increases economies of scale;
- Informs potential customers of new products;
- May detract from enjoyment of media (e.g. television);
- Revenue funds media (e.g. television);
- Tend to cancel each other out (adding to costs).

Advantages of advertising	Disadvantages of advertising

4.6 Profit maximisation

The diagram showing the long-run profit maximising position of a firm in monopolistic competition resembles that for a monopoly. As the firm has some control over price it cannot face a horizontal demand curve as it would in perfect competition. Therefore the demand curve is downward sloping left to right. It follows that its marginal revenue curve lies below that demand line. The average cost and marginal cost curves are the standard shape.

To profit maximise requires that the firm produces the output where marginal revenue equals marginal cost. The graph below shows the ***short-run*** equilibrium of a firm in monopolistic competition.

Unlike monopoly there are no barriers to entry so these super-profits cannot be maintained in the long-run, because competitors will enter the market and compete prices and profits downwards with close substitutes. Therefore, we have established the ***short-run*** equilibrium but not the long-run equilibrium of a profit maximising firm in monopolistic competition.

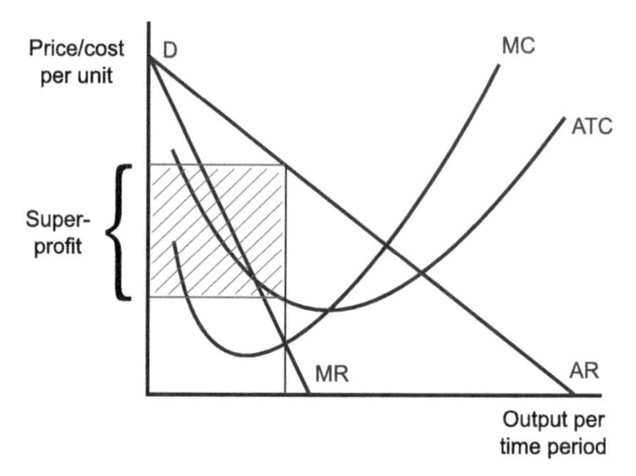

Short-run equilibrium of a firm in monopolistic competition

The long-run equilibrium has been illustrated in the diagram in 4.1 above .

Making a loss

Q9: It is possible that a firm operating in monopolistic competition may make a loss in the short-run.

Draw the diagram for such a position to show where losses would be minimised rather than profits maximised.

Hint: Move the cost curves. You will need ATC to be above AR if a loss is happening.

4.7 Summary

Summary

At the end of this topic students should know that:

- monopolistic competition is a market structure that lies between the theoretical extremes of perfect competition and monopoly;
- characteristics of monopolistic competition include the existence of many firms trying to market branded products using product differentiation;
- there are so many firms in the market that collusion between a few of them would have little impact on the overall market and is hence unlikely;
- companies spend heavily on marketing and advertising to increase market share and reduce price elasticity;
- in monopolistic competition, firms face a downward sloping demand curve with some influence over their prices. They are not price takers of perfect competition;
- the monopolistic competitor does not produce at the lowest point on the average total cost curve. They have higher costs than the perfect competitor;
- in monopolistic competition, super-profits and sub-normal profits are both possible in the short-run. The arrival of new competitors with substitute goods or the disappearance of the least efficient will return the market to a long-run equilibrium of normal profit.

4.8 End of topic test

End of Topic 4 test Go online 

Q10: A market structure in which many firms produce differentiated products is referred to as:

a) perfect competition.
b) monopoly.
c) monopolistic competition.
d) oligopoly.

....

Q11: Product differentiation can be achieved through:

a) the use of brand names and the use of packaging.
b) the use of brand names and variations in colour and style.
c) the use of packaging and variations in colour and style.
d) the use of brand names, the use of packaging and variations in colour and style.

....

Q12: Compared to monopoly, firms operating under monopolistic competition typically have more:

a) substitutes.
b) substitutes and economies of scale.
c) substitutes and control over price.
d) economies of scale and control over price.

....

Q13: Under monopolistic competition short-run super profits cannot be maintained in the long-run because:

a) average costs increase over time.
b) competitors can enter the market with close substitutes.
c) the demand line is horizontal.
d) lower prices are needed to increase sales.

....

Q14: Typically in monopolistic competition:

a) there is collusion among firms.
b) firms have no control over their prices.
c) each firm has only a small share of the market.
d) a few large firms dominate.

Q15: Compare and contrast monopolistic competition with perfect competition. *(10 marks)*

Hints: Compare the number and size of sellers, the influence over price, profitability in the short-run and in the long-run, the economic efficiency, and the level of barriers to entry.

Unit 1 Topic 5

Oligopoly

Contents

Learning objective

By the end of this topic students should be able to:

- define oligopoly;
- explain the characteristics of oligopolistic markets;
- explain the shape of the kinked demand curve facing an oligopolist;
- show an understanding of game theory;
- describe examples of markets that illustrate oligopoly.

5.1 Defining oligopoly

Oligopoly is a term used to describe a market that is dominated by a few large firms. The products of oligopolists are branded and hence differentiated from each other. However the basic products tend to be very similar, and differentiated largely through marketing effort.

The word oligopoly derives from the Greek word "oligos" meaning "few". The gulf between the theoretical market structure extremes of monopoly and perfect competition has been filled with two market structure models that are both very common in the real world. Oligopoly occupies a position on the market structure continuum nearer to monopoly than monopolistic competition and hence further from perfect competition.

A lot of theory suggests that oligopolies have the potential to stymy competition, and this does hold up well with regard to price competition. However, there are also many real examples of fierce **non-price competition** and considerable product innovation in oligopolistic markets. For the consumer there may be benefits as well as costs.

Oligopoly is a very common market form that lies between monopoly and monopolistic competition. One measure of the degree to which a market is an oligopoly is the **four-firm concentration ratio**. This establishes the market share held by the largest four suppliers to a particular market. There may, of course, be markets where concentration ratios of three, five or six firms offer more insight into the market situation. However the four-firm concentration ratio is often quoted and has become to some extent the standard measure of oligopoly.

Duopoly is a market structure where the two-firm concentration ratio, the market share held by two firms, is particularly high. It is similar to oligopoly and can be viewed as a specific type of oligopoly.

Types of market structure Go online 

Q1: Place the five types of market structure from the following list into the table below:

- duopoly;
- monopolistic competition;
- monopoly;
- oligopoly;
- perfect competition.

Number of sellers	Market structure
one	
two	
few	
many	
unlimited	

Oligopoly background reading Go online 

Use a search engine for "oligopoly" and find some background reading on the internet. You may also wish to refer to Tutor2u (https://www.tutor2u.net/) or Economics Help (http://bit.ly/1PJN7X5) .

Make notes from your reading on a word document. Consider printing these out for your folder. Alternatively you may wish to save your findings on computer or to memory stick.

5.2 Characteristics of oligopolistic markets

The following are typical features of a market in **oligopolistic competition**:

- a few firms dominate the market (not as many as in monopolistic competition) but there may also be a large number of smaller firms who do not have the ability to influence price.
- a few large firms have a large share of the total market for that product;
- an effort to differentiate your product from other similar products of the same type;
- significant barriers to entry exist and these are the key to continued above-normal profits in these industries;
- the decisions of one firm are made in the light of decisions made by the other firms in the market. This is termed "game theory" - reacting to or second-guessing the behaviour of other firms;
- non-price competition is the preferred way of competing for market share, although price wars can break out;
- price leadership, in which the prices set by one of the market leaders are tacitly adopted by its rivals, can occur;
- there is a constant threat of collusion and the forming of illegal cartels to share out the market and arrange prices that are very profitable for all.

Characteristics of oligopolistic markets Go online

Q2: Price competition is typical.

a) True
b) False

....

Q3: The entry of new firms into the market is difficult.

a) True
b) False

....

Q4: Game theory describes how firms react to the actions of competitors.

a) True
b) False

....

Q5: High spending on marketing is typical.

a) True
b) False

....

Q6: All firms produce an identical product.

a) True
b) False

....

Q7: The market is dominated by a few large firms.

a) True
b) False

5.3 Examples of oligopoly

There are many examples of firms operating in this market structure. We have established that, when considering the level of concentration of market share for a particular type of product, domination by a few large firms is the best way to identify oligopoly. Oligopolies can also be observed in local geographic areas in some industries.

For our general purposes there is little point in focusing on a precise figure for market concentration as these will inevitably be subject to variation over time. One suggested four-firm concentration ratio above which a market could be considered an oligopoly is 40%. Here are some recent approximate four-firm concentration ratios which fall into the 40% and above category:

- soaps and detergents - over 60%;
- greeting cards - over 80%;
- cigarettes - over 90%.

In 2014, the division of the UK supermarkets' market share figures for the top four firms was:

- Tesco - 29%;
- Asda - 17%;
- Sainsbury's - 16%;
- Morrisons - 11%.

This gave a four-firm concentration of 73%. Despite the existence of barriers to entry, new competitors from abroad (e.g. Aldi, Lidl) are taking business away from the major firms.

The four-firm concentration ratio for the European car market in 2014 was 53% and was broken down as follows:

- Volkswagen - 25%;
- PSA Peugeot Citroën - 12%;
- Renault - 9%;
- Ford - 7%.

The following table shows examples of brands operating in oligopolistic markets.

BMW	Ford	Airbus	Microsoft
Morrisons	RBS	PSA Peugeot Citroën	Procter & Gamble
Fiat	HSBC	Tesco	Asda
The Coca-Cola Company	General Motors	Lloyds Banking Group	Toyota
Volkswagen	Barclays	Hyundai	Sainsburys
Apple	Burger King	Nissan	KFC
B&Q	Renault	Homebase	PepsiCo
McDonald's	Boeing	Daimler AG	Unilever

Examples of brands operating in oligopolistic markets

Brands operating in oligopolistic markets

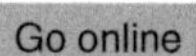

Q8: Within the table of brand names above are four examples of duopolies where the two-firm concentration ratio is very high.

In the table below, match the four pairs of companies with the oligopolistic markets listed.

Aircraft manufacture	
Soft drink manufacture	
Consumer goods	
Computer systems	

....

Q9: Within the table of brand names above are several examples of oligopolies.

In the table below, match the company names or brands with their oligopolistic market.

Automotive industry	
Banking	
Fast food restaurants	
DIY stores	
Supermarkets	

5.4 The kinked demand curve

The **kinked demand curve** that theoretically faces an oligopolist is illustrated below.

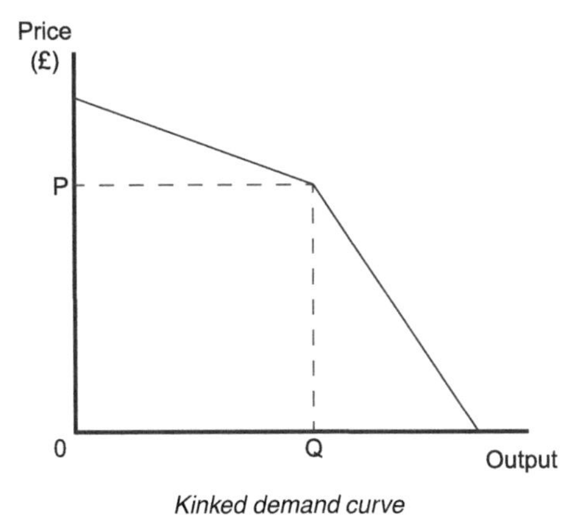

Kinked demand curve

When an oligopolist attempts to increase prices above the currently established price of P, the other firms will see an opportunity to increase their market share by not following this lead, or just by delaying in following this lead. Hence a small rise in price above P will lead to a substantial fall in customers and a transfer of market share to the other oligopolists.

When an oligopolist attempts to decrease prices below the currently established price of P, the other firms will probably respond by following the price reduction for fear of losing market share. Hence a small cut in price below P will lead to minimal gains in market share because most of the competitors will attempt to present consumers with a similar deal. The end result will be lower revenues and profits for all firms following a round of price cuts, and the same market share being fiercely maintained but at less profit.

Thus a price war is not a favoured option for oligopolists. It is recognised by operators in the industry as a lose-lose position for the companies. The gains go to the consumers. The demand curve is more price-elastic for price increases and less price elastic for price decreases.

Kinked demand curve video Go online 

At the time of writing a video on kinked demand curve theory lasting less than five minutes is available on YouTube - https://youtu.be/5BQPx8SL9F4 . You might find this alternative presentation of the kinked demand curve useful for consolidation.

When gas and electricity prices soared in 2008 some firms delayed the inevitable price rise. In return, they took a short term "hit" on profit margins but hoped to regain profit when newly acquired customers remained with them. This is fairly typical of oligopoly and is a response to the behaviour of other companies, in keeping with "game theory". Companies are setting their prices with a watchful eye on what the opposition are doing and behaving tactically to gain an edge.

Energy company price rise Go online 

Use the internet to find out the different price increases made by energy companies in the summer of 2008. Try searching for "centrica price rises 2008". Some articles may point out the motives of those firms that delayed or restricted price increases. In particular Centrica raised prices dramatically; how did their rivals react?

Non-price competition 

Q10: Make a list of the number of ways in which oligopolistic firms may compete without resorting to price cuts. For a context you could use UK supermarkets, e.g. Tesco, Asda, Morrisons, Sainsburys.

5.5 Game theory

In oligopoly all companies are interdependent and the directors of each company must take into account the likely tactics and responses of the opposing firms to any decision they might make. **Game theory** is the name given by economists to the study of this type of decision-making.

Game theory video Go online 

At the time of writing a short video on game theory is available on YouTube - https://youtu.be/JMq059SAQXM .

The prisoners' dilemma Go online 

Research the "prisoners' dilemma" using a search engine. The prisoners' dilemma shows why it is difficult to maintain cooperative behaviour although it is in the interests of all parties to do so.

The type of dilemma outlined in game theory can be illustrated by the table below. For the sake of simplicity we apply the game to a duopoly, but it could be widened to several firms.

	Firm B with current prices	**Firm B with price reduction**
Firm A with current prices	Firm A makes £100 profit	Firm A makes £10 profit
	Firm B makes £100 profit	Firm B makes £110 profit
Firm A with price reduction	Firm A makes £110 profit	Firm A makes £25 profit
	Firm B makes £10 profit	Firm B makes £25 profit

In this example, if one firm chooses to cut its prices then the additional sales will generate profits that increase by 10% to £110. However, the loss of market share leaves the other firm with under-utilised capital equipment and its profits slump by 90% to £10. If the second firm follows the lead on price reductions, both firms maintain market share but at the reduced prices have cut their profits to 25% of former levels.

Against this sort of background it is hardly surprising that price wars are not common in an oligopolistic market structure. Both firms rely on the behaviour of the other which can lead to collusion.

Tacit collusion

Tacit collusion occurs when all managers understand their market structure and realise that price cuts will merely rock the boat and act only in the consumers' interests. There is no reason for contact between the firms and no illegal collusion takes place. Typically one of the major firms becomes a "price leader" and the others gradually amend their catalogue to fall into line, including the maintaining of small differentials among different brands of basically the same product.

Notions of competition are kept alive as at least through the advertising agencies employed by the firms who compete to produce a winning advertisement that raises market share for their client firm. New products and brand extensions can be wheeled out periodically and competitions and special offers are acceptable tactics. Price cuts would be the last thing in mind - a beggar-thy-neighbour policy with unfortunate ramifications for all.

Cartels may be formed if price leadership and tacit collusion fail to inspire confidence among the firms. These are illegal and when found out can give rise to companies paying huge fines.

European Commission fines Go online 

Find out how much the European Commission has fined the companies involved in an alleged cartel for suppliers of vehicle glass.

Use a search engine for "cartel pilkington vehicle glass" for articles about this case. Find at least two further examples of cartels that have been prosecuted.

5.5.1 Competition and Markets Authority (CMA)

The Competition and Markets Authority (CMA) is an independent public body in the UK which conducts in-depth enquiries into mergers, markets and the regulation of the major regulated industries. The CMA website (https://www.gov.uk/cma) provides information such as current investigations and an archive of enquiries.

The four-firm concentration ratio for banks dealing in current accounts (2014) was over 77% of the market: Lloyds, RBS, HSBC, and Barclays. Additionally, much of the remaining market share went to Santander and Nationwide.

Lloyds Bank, Halifax (http://bit.ly/1EAAJjl) by Tim Green (http://bit.ly/199teER) is licensed under CC by 2.0 (http://bit.ly/17p9WuW)

An example of a CMA investigation into the UK banking industry, taken from a CMA press release (http://bit.ly/1MJPRip), is shown below:

'Personal current account and small business banking face full competition investigation

The CMA has today announced its decision to launch an in-depth market investigation into the personal current account and SME retail banking sectors, confirming its provisional decision of 18 July 2014.

The investigation will be conducted by a Market Reference Group drawn from the Competition and Markets Authority's (CMA) panel of independent members.

Following the announcement in July, the CMA embarked on a consultation regarding its provisional decision to launch a market investigation. Most respondents agreed that there should be a market investigation. Having carefully considered the consultation responses, the CMA continues to have concerns about the effectiveness of competition in these sectors and has decided to make a market investigation reference. These concerns include:

- *low levels of customers shopping around and switching;*
- *limited transparency, and difficulties for customers in making comparisons between banks, particularly for complex overdraft charges on personal current accounts;*
- *continuing barriers to entry and expansion into the sector, limiting the ability of smaller and newer providers to develop their businesses;*
- *very little movement over time in the market shares of the 4 largest banks, which provide over three-quarters of personal and business current accounts.*

Alex Chisholm, CMA Chief Executive, said: "Effective competition in retail banking is critically important for individual bank customers, small and medium-sized businesses, and the wider economy."'

5.5.2 Price fixing

The following example of price fixing is an extract from an article on fixing washing powder prices taken from the BBC Business website - http://bbc.in/1BUI51y :

> *"The consumer products giants Unilever and Procter & Gamble (P&G) have been fined 315m euros (£280m, $456m) for fixing washing powder prices in eight European countries. It follows a three-year investigation by the European Commission following a tip-off by the German company, Henkel.*
>
> *Unilever sells Omo and Surf, P&G makes Tide, and Henkel sells Persil in certain European countries.*
>
> *The fines were discounted by 10% after the two admitted running a cartel. Unilever was fined 104m euros and P&G was fined 211.2m euros. Henkel was not fined in return for providing the tip-off."*

Price fixing Go online 

Use a search engine to find some background on price fixing in the airline industry (between British Airways and Virgin Atlantic) and price fixing in the dairy industry.

5.6 Summary

Summary

At the end of this topic students should know that:

- oligopoly is a market structure that lies between the theoretical extremes of perfect competition and monopoly. Many industries exhibit the characteristics of oligopolistic competition;
- in oligopoly a few large firms dominate the market for a particular type of product. If the largest four firms have more than 40% of the market share then the market may be termed oligopolistic;
- an oligopolist faces a kinked demand curve. Raising price results in a great loss of customers to rivals (high price elasticity) but if price is lowered then rivals do the same and demand is not much increased (low price elasticity);
- game theory is one attempt by economists to develop a theory for the behaviour of oligopolistic markets;
- tacit collusion occurs when firms accept price leadership from one of the larger companies and choose to compete on non-price factors, such as product development and marketing activity;
- the small number of firms present in oligopolies gives rise to the danger of collusion to fix prices and share markets. When collusion is organised and there is concealed contact between the companies this is called a cartel and is illegal. There are many examples of investigations into oligopolies by regulatory bodies such as the European Commission and the Competition and Markets Authority (CMA).

5.7 End of topic test

End of Topic 5 test Go online 

Q11: Select the correct options from the text in italics in the following paragraph.

An oligopolistic market is dominated by (*1 / 5 / 50*) firms. They produce (*identical / differentiated*) products. (*Price / Non-price*) competition is the typical form of competition. Expenditure on advertising is often (*small / large*). The largest four firms could share (*15% / 50%*) of the market. The largest firm may offer price (*leadership / discounts*). Any price increase is likely to result in a price (*elastic / inelastic*) response because other firms hold their prices. This reactive behaviour is termed (*chaos / game*) theory.

....

Q12: Explain how firms compete in an oligopolistic market. *(10 marks)*

Hint: There are probably three sections to this answer:

1. *Explain briefly why price competition is not favoured;*
2. *Outline the non-price ways used;*
3. *Outline the importance of "game theory" in understanding oligopoly behaviour.*

Unit 1 Topic 6

Market failure

Contents

Learning objective

By the end of this topic students should be able to:

- explain the meaning of market failure;
- explain public goods as an example of market failure;
- explain merit and demerit goods as examples of market failure;
- explain externalities as an example of market failure;
- explain monopolies as an example of market failure;
- describe and discuss examples of market failure.

6.1 The meaning of market failure

Market failure is the term used to describe markets that fail to function efficiently in the way they price or allocate goods. The market mechanism sets prices according to the laws of supply and demand. In some cases there is no market because the private business sector of the economy cannot supply some goods and services. In other cases the market works to an extent but the goods and services are priced too low or too high and the wrong quantities are produced.

The market may not provide goods in a fair (or equitable) way, leading to extremes of wealth and poverty. In this case, political parties in government make subjective decisions on the appropriate extent of re-distribution. A few right-wing free market economists will argue that the extremes of wealth and poverty reflect the contribution or activity of the players in the market. Most people will take the view that power in the market does not always match the size of contribution, ability or work of an individual and that there is a strong case for re-distributing from the rich to the poor, as long as this does not harm the incentives to participate in production.

We will look at the following examples of market failure:

- ***public goods***,
- ***merit goods***,
- ***demerit goods***,
- ***externalities***,
- ***monopolies***,
- ***factor markets***.

Market failure Go online 

Research the topic "market failure" on the internet, make your own notes based on this study and then answer the question below. You may also wish to refer to Tutor2u (https://www.tutor2u.net/) or Economics Help (http://bit.ly/1PJN7X5) .

Q1: What is meant by the term "market failure"?

6.2 Public goods

Public goods cannot be provided by private enterprise. The problem is the impossibility of excluding non-payers from using the good or service. How can a profit be made from a product that cannot be fenced off from non-payers? This is best explained by an example.

Sophie arrives at the bottom of a steep hill which she must climb in order to get home. It is dark and the moon is behind a cloud. The streetlights will work if she puts £1 in the slot at the bottom of the hill - Sophie will then have ten minutes to get home. As soon as she sets off, a bus arrives and unloads five passengers who then walk up the hill for free.

How can a profit be made from providing street lights? It is too expensive and inconvenient to erect high fences and a turnstile on every corner. Anyway, how would the cars get through?
Street-lighting is a typical public good. Free riders (non-payers) cannot be easily excluded. Private business cannot then turn a profit and they would not be provided at all unless government steps in and pays for them using taxpayers' money.

Street lighting

Q2: If the street lighting is made available by the local council, does Sophie's use of the lights diminish their availability to others? Explain your answer.

Hint: you won't find the answer in the above section on non-excludability. As an advanced higher candidate you have been posed a problem that requires you to think up and explain another feature of public goods.

6.3 Merit and demerit goods

Merit goods can be provided by the market, but not in sufficient numbers. The private benefits are less than the social benefits. This can be shown diagrammatically (see diagram below).

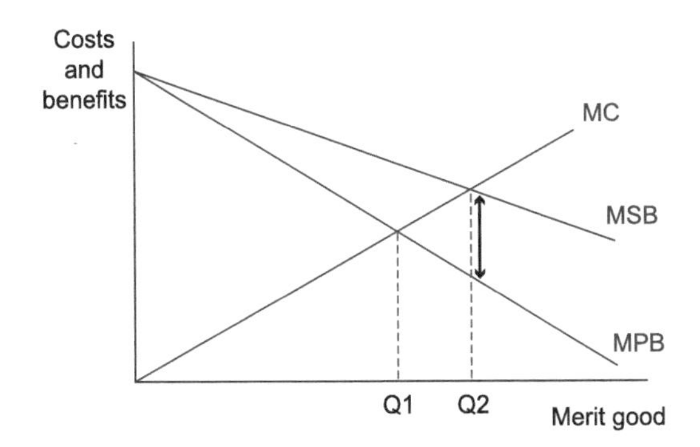

Marginal social benefits (MSB) compared with marginal private benefits (MPB) for a merit good

This diagram shows that marginal social benefits (MSB) exceed marginal private benefits (MPB) for a merit good such as education. The arrowed gap between marginal social benefits and marginal private benefits represents the marginal external (third party) benefits. While education creates private benefits, such as the opportunity to obtain a better job, it also creates social benefits.

One example of a wider social benefit may be the increased productivity and economic growth created in an economy of well-educated people. Thus a merit good has wider benefits for society on top of the private benefits. If it was available in a free market without government subsidy, only Q1 of education would be provided.

Merit goods are under-provided in this marketplace. The efficient use of scarce resources would involve a higher level of production at Q2 where the marginal cost (MC) equals the entire marginal social benefit and not just the benefit to the private purchaser. Private customers would pay only to the point where the marginal cost equalled the perceived marginal private benefit. There is a strong case for the state to subsidise education to reflect the marginal social benefits thus using valuable scarce resources to best advantage.

Demerit goods

Q3: Explain, ***using a diagram***, how negative externalities can lead to the over consumption of a **demerit good** such as whisky.

Hint: The diagram will have two lines rising from left to right representing marginal social cost and marginal private cost. A line representing marginal benefit will fall from left to right. Your explanation will turn around the above explanation for merit goods.

6.4 Externalities

Externalities are third-party costs or benefits resulting from a transaction. Externalities can result from production (e.g. pollution) or from consumption (e.g. anti-social behaviour).

The buyer and the seller are the first two parties and they agree a price to their mutual satisfaction. However, another party can be affected by their business activity.

One example of a positive externality could be the provision of public transport. This results in less congestion, less pollution, fewer accidents and potentially some savings on road building. This list of wider benefits that are not reflected in the fares charged can be used to make the case to subsidise public transport.

Negative externalities are very common. Large trucks could be considered to create external costs such as:

- delays to other road users arising from their slower speeds and their part in road congestion;
- noise pollution to citizens as they thump along the main streets of towns and villages where there is no bypass;
- air pollution that affects the general public and not just those buying the particular goods in the truck.

Negative externalities

Name the negative externalities associated with the following activities. Note that the answers below may not be exhaustive.

Q4: Drinking alcohol.

....

Q5: Driving gas-guzzling SUVs (also known as "Chelsea Tractors").

....

Q6: Smoking tobacco.

....

Q7: Tarring over your front garden to allow parking of vehicles.

Smoking - a merit or demerit good?

Q8: If smokers pay a lot more tax and die younger, therefore contributing more to government finances than they use up, would this make smoking a merit good instead of a demerit good?

Hint: this is an interesting and thought-provoking question requiring a clear understanding of the topic of externalities. Please give it some careful thought.

6.5 Monopolies

Monopoly, as a type of market, has been dealt with in detail in an earlier topic, so what follows is a summary of the problems that make it as much an example of a type of market failure as a type of market.

It is an irony of the capitalist system, driven by the profit motive, that firms can take this profit-seeking motive too far. As profit-maximisers, firms try to get rid of the opposition and charge consumers higher prices. Those that are most successful in the marketplace will come to dominate it and at that point the market fails.

A market fails if it is unable to deliver products efficiently. Economic efficiency requires that the prices faced by consumers reflect the true cost of the factors of production involved in the production process (price equal to marginal cost). If consumers are overcharged for a product then the opportunity cost of that product has increased, and the good is likely to be under-consumed. This is economically less efficient. The true cost of production would leave the factor, enterprise, with a normal profit rather than an above-normal profit.

Prices can be maintained above marginal cost in the long-run. The lack of any competition enables the monopolist to charge higher prices and make above-normal profits. Barriers to entry maintain this situation.

The simple diagram below illustrates how monopoly price (MP) tends to be higher than price (P) would be in a competitive market and monopoly output (MQ) tends to be lower than output (Q) would be in a competitive market.

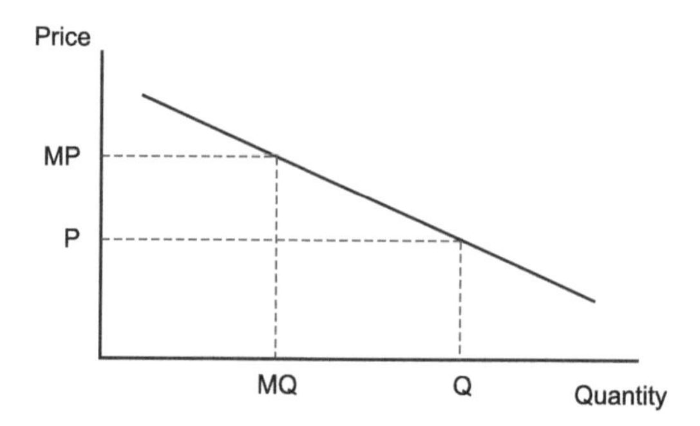

The effect of monopoly on price and output

Barriers to entry prevent the erosion by competitors of the high prices charged by the monopolist. Were it possible to allocate resources, as in a competitive market, the supply and consumption of the product would increase. Monopoly, therefore, causes a market failure through the misallocation of resources.

6.5.1 Barriers to entry

Barriers to entry are key to maintaining a monopoly. They make it difficult for new firms to move into the same market as an established monopoly.

Some examples of typical barriers to entry are:

- ***patents, trade marks and copyright restrictions*** which are legal rights to be the sole provider of a product for a period of time;
- ***licences and franchises granted by government*** which also offer an unchallenged market position for a period of time;
- ***economies of scale*** which can be vast and make it impossible for a new entrant to establish a low enough cost structure to enable it to compete. New firms trying to gain a foothold in the market are unable to match the low production costs and hence low customer prices of the established firm;
- ***start-up costs*** which can be a great disincentive to new firms. The initial capital investment required may be irrecoverable and have to be written-off if an adequate market share cannot be established quickly;
- ***existing brand loyalty and recognition by consumers*** which is difficult to overcome and will require expensive advertising and competitive pricing;
- ***predatory pricing by the established firm*** which may under-cut a new entrant and drive them out of business;
- ***vertically integrated firms*** that will enjoy a degree of control over raw materials, components, and market outlets. This could be because suppliers have been taken over, or happen through existing contractual arrangements.

Barriers to entry

Q9: Discuss the extent to which the company Microsoft could be said to benefit from barriers to entry.

Hint: for full marks a suitable approach would be to seek five distinct angles and discuss in five paragraphs. Alternatively, if using only three or four different starting points then the discussion would have to be deeper to obtain the marks.

6.6 Market failure in factor markets

We can extend our look at market failure away from the market for goods and services. In the **market for factors** of production, such as labour, the market can also fail to operate efficiently. Indeed, it may fail more regularly.

North-south divide

For a long period, in discussions on the UK economy in the 1980s and 1990s, the term "the north-south divide" came up frequently, especially in the press where simplification of complex economic concepts is needed for the layperson reader. This term in part describes a failure in the labour market.

In the poorer north there had been a long-term structural decline in mining and manufacturing industry. The products of these industries could be obtained more cheaply from abroad and their gradual loss of comparative advantage rendered them uncompetitive. The free market policies of Mrs Thatcher's government and a high exchange rate for sterling accelerated their decline with the government firmly opposed to subsidies and market intervention. In the richer south, newer sunrise industries and service-based employment had clustered in locations nearer to European markets.

Regional unemployment

Unemployment rates from that time illustrate how geographically lopsided the UK economy had become. The uneven distribution of unemployment that was sustained over many years points to market failure in the labour market.

Workers found it difficult to leave areas of high unemployment and seek work in more prosperous areas. The private housing market meant that moving south was expensive and prevented labour from moving to areas of labour shortage. Satisfactory social housing was even more difficult to find in these areas and moving location was effectively prevented. The private rented sector was small. Without intervention and assistance from government it was difficult for those in the north to move south for employment opportunities. This is geographic immobility of labour.

Retraining

Similarly the market did not provide information on job opportunities in an effective way, especially when these jobs were distant. The market failed to provide enough retraining opportunities. After all, a trained worker may find it easy to leave the company that trained her/him; hardly a reason for providing expensive training. Therefore, the government was left to intervene using taxpayers' money to attempt to do what the market failed to do. That is, relocate and retrain workers in sufficient numbers and increase the occupational mobility of the workforce.

Regional unemployment Go online 

Q10: Using the internet, find some figures for regional unemployment in the UK from the 1980s.

6.7 Summary

Summary

At the end of this topic students should know that:

- market failure is a broad term that describes markets that are unable to deliver goods and services in an efficient or equitable way. These markets left alone will fail to provide essential goods to the poor and over-supply goods with negative externalities;
- public goods cannot be profitably supplied by private firms because non-payers cannot be excluded from the benefits. e.g. street-lighting;
- merit goods have wider benefits for the community, e.g. education. Governments want to encourage widespread availability but private firms will only provide them for those who can pay;
- demerit goods have wider costs to the community, e.g. alcohol. Governments want to limit demand as unfettered markets are capable of supplying vast quantities of these goods at low prices;
- externalities are third-party costs, e.g. pollution. The market price reflects the costs of production but many products have negative externalities that are a cost to others not involved in the transaction;
- monopoly is an example of market failure as it is generally associated with costs such as higher prices and economic inefficiency. However it also conveys benefits such as vast economies of scale and investment in R&D;
- labour markets also illustrate market failure when unemployed workers are unable to smoothly relocate or retrain for jobs available in other regions or industries.

6.8 End of topic test

End of Topic 6 test Go online

Q11: Market failure describes markets that fail to:

a) find an equilibrium price.
b) allocate goods efficiently through the price mechanism.
c) Both of the above.
d) Neither of the above.

....

Q12: Public goods can be defined by:

a) the inability to exclude non-payers and under-provision by the market.
b) the inability to exclude non-payers and the unlimited availability for use by others.
c) under-provision by the market and the unlimited availability for use by others.
d) the inability to exclude non-payers, under-provision by the market and the use of the good does not limit its availability to others.

....

Q13: Positive externalities of rail travel could be:

a) fewer road accidents and less congestion.
b) fewer road accidents and less pollution.
c) less congestion and less pollution.
d) fewer road accidents, less congestion and less pollution.

....

Q14: Private enterprise seeks to maximise long-term:

a) profit.
b) social welfare.
c) output.
d) competition.

....

Q15: Select the list that contains a public good, a merit good, and a demerit good (or service) in that order.

a) Street lighting, education, alcohol
b) Health care, roads, tobacco
c) Insurance, health care, air travel
d) Education, health care, travel by private car

....

Q16: To encourage the smooth operation of the labour market, the government could:

a) subsidise the relocation of unemployed workers.
b) subsidise the relocation of unemployed workers and improve knowledge of vacancies.
c) improve knowledge of vacancies and leave retraining to private enterprise.
d) leave retraining to private enterprise.

....

Q17: Externalities are:

a) reflected in the producer's costs of production.
b) always negative but not reflected in the equilibrium price.
c) third party costs (or benefits) that fall on neither the buyer nor the seller.
d) built into the price by the market mechanism.

....

Q18: The production of merit goods is typically:

a) taxed by government.
b) subsidised by government.
c) licensed by government.
d) left to private enterprise.

....

Q19: Which of the following is an example of market failure?

a) Radioactive particles from nuclear power plant on a public beach and the noise from a "hen" party going home at 2am.
b) Radioactive particles from nuclear power plant on a public beach and the dominance of Sky TV in bidding for live football.
c) The noise from a "hen" party going home at 2am and the dominance of Sky TV in bidding for live football.
d) Radioactive particles from nuclear power plant on a public beach, the noise from a "hen" party going home at 2am and the dominance of Sky TV in bidding for live football.

....

Q20: Which of the following is an accurate statement?

a) For merit goods, the social benefits exceed the private benefits.
b) Public goods can only partly be provided by private enterprise.
c) Economic efficiency is guaranteed by the market mechanism.
d) Third party costs are reflected in the market price of goods.

Q21: Explain why in some cases markets cannot be relied upon to supply goods and services efficiently and in the quantities desired.

(20 marks)

Hint: This requires a careful explanation of issues surrounding public goods, merit goods, demerit goods and monopoly.

Unit 1 Topic 7

Government intervention

Contents

Learning objective

By the end of this topic students should be able to:

- discuss whether or not government should intervene;
- explain the various intervention options available to government;
- describe and discuss various examples of government intervention.

7.1 Should governments intervene?

At one extreme of the political spectrum are those who find the operation of capitalist markets so inequitable that they would prefer **government to intervene** and take over the production and allocation of goods and services. They may be called communists and the type of centralised state-run economy that they advocate can be termed a centrally planned economy.

At the other extreme are those whose belief in the efficacy of markets is quasi-religious. These free marketeers (those in favour of free market solutions) have a Darwinesque economic view, tied up with a belief in individual freedoms, that a stronger economy emerges as only the strongest thrive. The consequence of this tends to be that the weakest and those who make poor decisions are not rescued by the state and instead rely on charity.

Despite apparent problems with largely unregulated markets, free marketeers will often claim that it is more **deregulation** that these markets need. They see the market as the best mechanism for allocating resources, goods and services to the areas where consumers indicate they are wanted. Entrepreneurs, striving for efficiency and profit and responding to consumers, are more likely to achieve an optimal outcome than government bureaucrats attempting to predict public wants.

Free marketeers seek minimal government intervention, e.g. to provide security, public goods and, perhaps, some merit goods and prevent the creation of monopolies. The faults of markets, they would claim, are caused by the incapability of governments to stay out of them.

The vast majority of economists are much more pragmatic than these two extremes. They see the faults of laissez faire markets and the faults of centrally planned alternatives. They look for a functioning middle road rather than worshipping theoretical extremes.

Free markets Go online 

Go on to the internet and carry out some research on free markets. You may also wish to refer to Tutor2u (https://www.tutor2u.net/) or Economics Help (http://bit.ly/1PJN7X5) .

Adam Smith's concept 

Q1: Supporters of free markets believe that resources are most efficiently allocated when economic decisions are made in a decentralised way by individuals. To what extent does Adam Smith's concept of the "invisible hand" support this idea. (In order to answer this question you could use the internet to access the text of "The Wealth of Nations" by Adam Smith.)

7.1.1 Economic intervention

The market place does not care about the merit of the goods and services to society. For example, consumers might spend money on trivial items while fellow citizens freeze in winter. The market is inanimate, has no opinion and makes no value judgements.

Without intervention, power in the marketplace creates extremes of wealth and poverty that appear to owe little to the effort expended or the quality of that effort. Family wealth and power can be maintained through increasingly indolent generations hiring accountants, for example, to manage investments and avoid paying tax.

Interventionists, unlike free market devotees, expect the market to fail with great regularity but would rather the market attempted to allocate resources and goods in the first instance. They accept that producers seeking to maximise profits and consumers seeking to maximise utility is an excellent starting point for the mixed economy outcome they propose. They also accept that there is an underlying efficiency to the basic operation of the market.

Interventionists intervene to smooth the operation of the market economy, to remove the harsh, rough edges. Interventionists do not generally go so far as to seek a centrally planned economy. We now have historical data on how inefficient and corrupt these economies were in the twentieth century and they have now largely reinvented themselves using market principles.

Economic intervention 

Go on to the internet and carry out some research on economic intervention. As a result of your research, you should be able to list examples of economic intervention.

7.2 Income redistribution

Without a process for **redistributing income and wealth** it is likely that the gap between rich and poor would widen. A wealthy person would not seem to have much to gain by accepting that some of his/her wealth should be recycled to poorer people, but consider the following benefits to them:

- If the poor were unable to afford basic health care then illnesses often associated with poverty, such as tuberculosis, would thrive. It is unlikely they could avoid contact with the less well off to the extent that such contagions would not reach them.
- On their way to an expensive city restaurant they may have to step over the poor living in cardboard boxes or pass impoverished street children begging for money and it might affect the enjoyment of their night out.

- They face an increased risk of being mugged on the way home as poverty will incline some towards crime. When they arrive home, they might pass through an expensive security gate into a walled grounds watched over by CCTV. When shopping in the mall, armed private security guards might be used to keep the poor out.

Poor man begging for money from a wealthy man

This might seem far-fetched but the shanty town dwellers on the edge of South American cities are not welcome in the shopping malls of the prosperous. Also, especially on the back of drug culture, diseases such as tuberculosis can thrive in parts of apparently rich countries such as the United States.

So, even if you are wealthy, and have no moral scruples or questions over the fairness of your good fortune, it may benefit you to see that the living conditions and aspirations of the poor are raised. On the other hand it might suit you better to let other rich people pay and take care of this for you, and head for Monaco or some other tax haven with a free ride on the back of the moral rich. Consider that in the UK it is possible to receive honours (knighthoods, OBEs, etc.) while making sure your wealth is hidden from HM Revenue and Customs!

To assuage those extremes of wealth and poverty, governments tend to use **progressive tax** systems. This is aimed at achieving a fairer distribution of income. "Fairer" is not an objective term, so economists must make subjective value judgements. In a democratic system, elected politicians will have a mandate to bring about their definition of fairness and employed economists will explain to them how to make it happen.

Those on lower incomes will have a higher marginal propensity to consume. If money is re-distributed towards them, then aggregate demand may increase leading to higher economic growth.

Income redistribution Go online 

Q2: There are many moral reasons for income re-distribution but suggest two reasons arising from self-interest.

7.2.1 Progressive tax systems

Progressive tax systems take a higher percentage of income from the rich than from the poor. The poor also tend to benefit more from the public spending of government. Thus, by the way government raises funds and by the way it spends them, the poor tend to be beneficiaries and income is redistributed.

Income tax

Income tax is an excellent example of a progressive tax system having a standard rate and a higher rate. Indeed, there is a case for it having more than two higher rates and three bands.

UK Income Tax rates and allowances (in February 2015) are shown in the graph below:

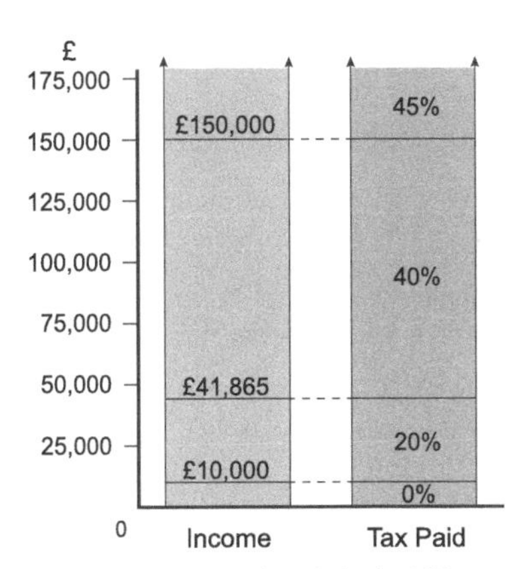

Income tax bands in the UK
Source: https://www.gov.uk/income-tax-rates

For standard personal allowances, as of February 2015:

- income up to £10,000 is tax free. Most people start paying basic rate tax on taxable income over £10,000;
- the basic rate of tax was 20%, for income up to £31,865. Most people start paying higher rate tax on income over £41,865, because the first £10,000 is tax-free;
- the higher rate of tax was 40%, for income up to £150,000;

- the additional rate of tax was 45%, for income over £150,000.

State education

The provision of state education may be universal but those who are better off may choose to send their children to private schools ("public schools" is the misleading term used in England). Thus the benefit of free schooling is not necessarily taken up by the rich and therefore can be an example of state spending being progressive and benefiting those on lower incomes. However, if a local council subsidises a theatre and that theatre is more regularly used by the middle classes, then this state spending could be said to be regressive.

Wealth tax

In some countries a wealth tax exists, so that the pile of capital accumulated over the years and centuries can be taxed as well as the annual income. The UK has no wealth tax, but perhaps the nearest is the tax on property that provides local councils with funds. Many people in the UK put a large proportion of their wealth into their property, so a system that taxes big houses more than small houses is similar to a tax on wealth.

A closer analysis of the benefits of government spending is required to back up the assertion that the poor benefit more, and equally the assertion that the very rich fund these benefits. That would be outside the remit of this course. **Transfers** can be universal and are not always aimed at the poor. Equally there is little scope for tax avoidance for those employed in the professions and they bear the burden of progressive income tax while the very wealthy with tax accountants find loop-holes that allow them to avoid much tax.

UK income tax Go online

Use the internet to answer the following questions.

Q3: Find out the current structure of income tax in the UK. At what point do people start paying tax? At what point do they pay the higher rate?

....

Q4: What was the UK top rate of income tax in 1974?

....

Q5: How does the current top rate of income tax in the UK compare to other countries?

7.3 Provision of public goods

We have already established in a previous topic that the state must provide public goods as by definition the market will not be able to.

Consider what would happen if the market provided a fire service. An insurance firm would decide to protect insured properties by having its own private fire brigade. A fire at an uninsured property or at a property insured by a different company would not be the insurance company's problem. It might be sensible to come to agreements with other companies so that the brigades could help each other, although it could be tricky working out how much each firm should pay into this combined brigade.

What if a fire started in an uninsured property along the street from an insured one? Would you wait until it is next door before starting to hose down insured properties, or would you end up intervening earlier and protecting a number of uninsured premises to prevent the insured property catching light? There would be a number of free riders close to the insured property. Without paying they receive the benefit of fire cover. If many do not pay, then the chance of making sufficient revenue to operate the service is reduced and it becomes a case of market failure - a case of a public good.

Provision of public goods

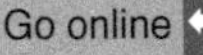

Use the internet to answer the questions.

Q6: Decide which of the following goods and services are provided mainly by the UK Government, the private sector or by both sectors and put them into the correct column in the table below:

- Cars;
- Education;
- Electricity;
- Health services;
- Keep fit classes;
- Police;
- Refuse collection;
- Roads;
- School cleaning;
- Streetlights;
- Water.

Government	Private	Partly private

Q7: So which of the above items are public goods under the definition of being unable to exclude non-payers?

7.4 Licences and regulation

Licences and regulations are often used in the area of demerit goods. Age restrictions and limitations on opening times are common. The provision of such goods and services may require a licence application to be passed and such licences can be withdrawn if the regulations are not complied with.

Sometimes it is only permissible to consume such goods and services on licensed premises. In some cases the regulations will ban certain goods and services, making their sale and consumption illegal. In these ways the government limits or controls the consumption of demerit goods.

Q8: Can you think of an example of licences and regulations?

....

Q9: Can you think of an example of a banned good?

Regulations may place a limit on the amount of negative externalities that can be produced. Controls can be placed on the emissions from power stations or the waste products that can be piped into a river. The good being produced is still being produced but without so many negative externalities, and the polluter is paying for the filters and controls. Then the consumer will pay a price closer to the true social cost of producing the good when the additional costs are passed on.

Laws can also be useful to require positive externalities to be produced. When a local planning authority requires that the external appearance of a building be aesthetically pleasing or just fits in with its surroundings, it is requiring that the owner or builder makes a product that generates positive external benefits for the community (or at least does not provide negative externalities).

Positive and negative externalities Go online 

Q10: Decide which of the following scenarios give rise to positive or negative externalities for the wider community and put them into the correct column in the table below:

- Decorating the outside of your house with 2,000 flashing lights at Christmas;
- Driving at 100mph;
- Keeping your front garden neat;
- Partying in the street at 3am;
- Smoking cigarettes;
- Vaccinating your child against measles.

Positive externalities	Negative externalities	Both positive and negative externalities

7.5 Taxation

Taxation is a favoured choice of market adjustment for governments. Tax makes up for the difference between the price being based on private costs and the price that reflects the social costs including negative externalities.

Consumers will now be able to make their mind up on the purchases they make in a marketplace that has somewhat adjusted for negative externalities. At higher prices they will buy less, so less will be made of products that create negative externalities. The sales of products that entail negative externalities will now reflect the true cost to the community to a greater extent.

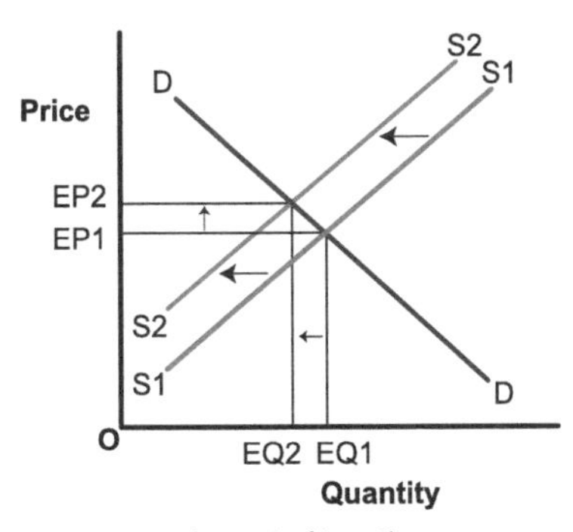

Impact of taxation

A tax moves supply leftwards, and less is sold at the higher price. The tax will impact on producers who will sell less and on consumers who pay more.

This can only help in the efficient allocation of resources, as false signals sent due to market failure have been amended by the imposition of an appropriate tax.

Taxation means the firm responsible for the creation of negative externalities will now have to pay some of the third-party costs. This is the principle that the polluter should pay.

Current levels of taxation Go online 

Q11: Use the internet to find out the current level of tax on:

- a bottle of wine;
- a litre of petrol;
- 20 cigarettes.

7.6 Subsidies

Subsidies can be thought of as negative taxation. Instead of forcing the market price upwards, they allow it to be cut. This ensures that more merit goods are produced and consumed. Merit goods can then be priced in a way that reflects their additional value to the community over and above what the private user pays.

Subsidies encourage the production of merit goods, such as education and health care. Merit goods would otherwise be under-produced because the market price does not reflect the gain to the community from their production. Subsidies can also be used by governments to subvert market outcomes, as in the case of the EU sugar subsidy that advantages EU farmers.

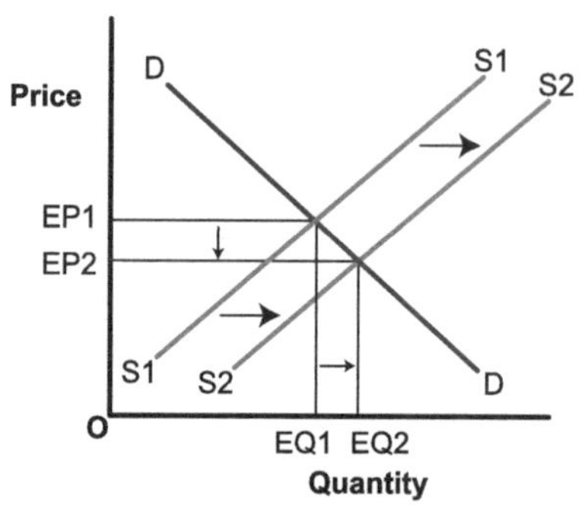

Impact of subsidies

A subsidy moves supply rightwards. This encourages the production of more to satisfy the higher demand at the reduced price.

Subsidies Go online 

Q12: Decide which of the following goods and services are generally subsidised or not subsidised within the UK. and put them into the correct column in the table below:

- Diesel cars;
- Education;
- Eye tests;
- Medicines;
- Museums;
- Newspapers;
- Orchestras;
- Rail travel;
- Rural bus routes;
- Sugar.

Subsidised	Not subsidised

7.7 Government and monopoly

The allocation of resources would more reflect the wishes of the consumer if monopolies were prevented and goods were priced appropriately.

Monopoly leads to higher prices and the exploitation of the consumer who must pay higher prices for goods bought in uncompetitive markets. These higher prices mean that the good is consumed to a lesser extent than if the price was set in a competitive market. Therefore, there is a misallocation of resources by the market, as if it had operated properly the lower price would have led to higher consumption and the devotion of more resources to the good's production. The market cannot truly reflect the consumers' wishes when it sets false prices. This is an example of market failure.

Economic efficiency requires that the prices faced by consumers reflect the true cost of the factors of production involved in the production process (price equal to marginal cost). If consumers are overcharged for a product then the opportunity cost of that product has increased, and the good is likely to be under-consumed. This is economically less efficient. The true cost of production would leave the factor, enterprise, with a normal profit, not an above-normal profit.

Monopoly also fails because it provides less choice for consumers, and there is less need for it to innovate.

Q13: Summarise how monopolies have an adverse effect on economic efficiency.

7.7.1 Competition and Markets Authority (CMA)

The issue of monopoly has been addressed in a variety of ways:

- Refusing take-overs and mergers that would reduce competition,
- Setting up agencies that monitor the prices and performance of monopolies,
- Taking monopolies into state ownership (nationalisation),
- Breaking-up monopolies into smaller independent companies,

- De-regulating markets alongside privatisation of monopolies.

Mergers that give market control to the newly-merged company are generally referred to the **Competition and Markets Authority**. If *Tesco* were to attempt to take-over any of the other large supermarket chains (e.g. *Morrisons*) it would be extremely likely to be refused. *Tesco* has such a share of supermarket sales in the UK that it can only expand overseas or into other product areas.

OFGEM is the regulatory body set up to monitor the performance and prices of the energy companies. It has to be satisfied that the prices charged to consumers are not excessive and the rate of return for shareholders is not abnormally high. In the water industry where substantial investment to replace ageing infrastructure and improve standards has been required, the regulatory body has allowed significant price rises when the revenues are allocated to meeting higher standards.

Competition and Markets Authority (CMA) Go online 

Go to the CMA website (https://www.gov.uk/cma) and examine the work of the Competition and Markets Authority. Investigate some of the reports in the archive section.

7.7.2 Nationalisation versus privatisation

Nationalisation in the UK is out of fashion or, some would say, discredited. Until the 1980s large parts of UK industry were state-owned - gas, electricity and railways to name only three. Textbooks referred to these areas as natural monopolies, implying that the only efficient way to run them was as one massive company generating enormous economies of scale. In theory the competitive alternative would have had higher unit costs and been less efficient, because it would have been uneconomic to replicate expensive infrastructure.

The option of nationalising a monopoly, especially where taxpayer subsidies are huge, has not gone away. Recently Network Rail, who maintain the railway infrastructure, were effectively nationalised, although the very word "nationalisation" has such negative connotations that politicians found a new way of describing it.

Rarely, monopolies have been broken up. Historical US examples include the break-up of the original Standard Oil into 34 smaller oil companies in 1911. The broken-up company gave birth to Exxon, Amoco, Chevron and Mobil among others. Some might have made a case for Microsoft to go the same way, but this now seems unlikely to happen.

The deregulation of a market often follows the privatisation of a state monopoly. Monopolies are dealt with by creating a competitive market place. State monopolies were broken up to introduce an element of competition to markets, which was expected to drive down costs and improve efficiency.

Deregulation of the bus industry

One example of deregulation in the UK is the bus industry. Previously, timetabled services were a state monopoly. When the regional companies owned by the state were privatised, other private coach companies that had previously only been allowed to offer tours and excursions were allowed to apply for timetabled routes. Over a short period most of the competitors were eliminated and the market came to be dominated by a few successful firms such as Stagecoach and First Group. The market began to show the signs of oligopoly, and in many localities there was no significant competition. The big firms ensured that the smaller ones had difficulty operating in competition.

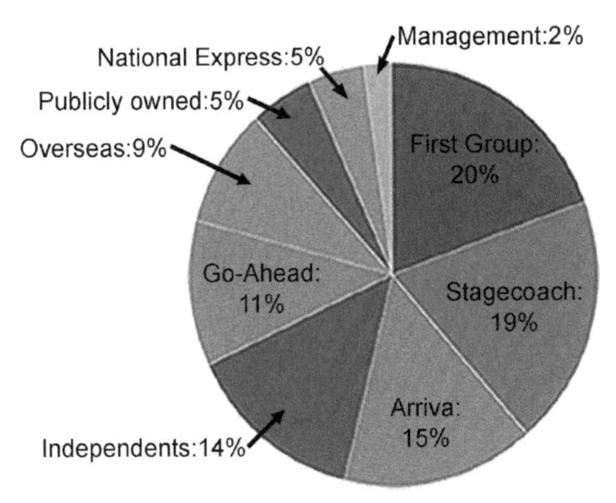

Data supplied courtesy of The TAS Partnership www.tas.uk.net.
Market share based on turnover of subsidies owned in 2010-11.

Source: Stagecoach website (http://bit.ly/1OZAfcF)

In 2012 the deregulated bus industry market share were as follows:

- First Group: 20%;
- Stagecoach: 19%;
- Arriva: 15%;
- Go-Ahead: 11%;
- National Express: 5%;
- Other: 30%.

This gives a four-firm concentration ratio in the bus industry of 65%. A search of the reports on the Competition and Markets Authority for matches with Stagecoach finds numerous matches - so clearly the Competition and Markets Authority is monitoring activity in the bus industry.

Regulatory bodies 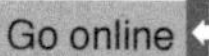 

Find out about the remit of these regulatory bodies by visiting their websites:

- Ofwat (http://www.ofwat.gov.uk);
- ORR (http://orr.gov.uk);
- Ofcom (http://www.ofcom.org.uk).

7.8 Summary

Summary

- The extent of government intervention in the market that is required is a matter of great debate among economists, some of whom advocate leaving the market largely unregulated, whereas other economists point to numerous examples of market failure and see a major role for government intervention.
- Government redistributes income and wealth through a progressive tax system that takes a higher percentage from the wealthy and then this money is recycled towards poorer families.
- Government intervenes to provide public goods by providing the good or service directly out of tax revenue.
- Laws can be passed to criminalise some goods, e.g. illegal drugs. Regulations can be used to limit negative externalities, e.g. enforcing filters on power station chimneys. Licences may be required to provide some goods and services, e.g. alcohol.
- Taxation can be used to amend upwards the market prices of demerit goods such as tobacco so that they reflect the true cost to the community of their production and consumption.
- Subsidies encourage the production of merit goods which would otherwise be under-produced. Subsidies can also be used by governments to subvert market outcomes.
- Monopolies charge higher prices and this leads to the under-production and under-consumption of the goods they put to market.

7.9 End of topic test

End of Topic 7 test Go online 

Q14: Match the correct government intervention terms from the following list to each description in the table below:

- CMA;
- Licences;
- Progressive taxes;
- Regulatory bodies;
- Subsidies;
- Taxes and duties.

Description	Government intervention
Checks on market domination	
Discourage demerit goods	
Encourage merit goods	
Monitors prices and services	
Redistribute income	
Required to operate	

....

Q15: Explain the difference between internal and external costs. *(SQA 2007)*

(2 marks)

....

Q16: Describe how the house planning system attempts to tackle the problems created by external costs. *(SQA 2007)*

(2 marks)

....

Q17: Describe the measures taken in the UK to limit the power of monopoly and oligopoly firms. Discuss the effectiveness of these measures? *(SQA 2007)*

(9 marks)

Unit 1 Topic 8

Economic markets tests

Economic markets test

Go online

Q1: Match the correct economic market terms from the following list to each description in the table below:

- Demerit good;
- Government intervention;
- Merit good;
- Monopolistic competition;
- Monopoly;
- Negative externality;
- Oligopoly;
- Perfect competition;
- Positive externality;
- Public good.

Description	Government intervention
A well-kept garden	
Dominated by a few large firms	
Non-payers cannot be excluded	
Only one firm in this industry	
Over-provided by the market	
Pollution from a factory chimney	
Products differentiated by design and colour	
Taxes, subsidies and licences	
Thousands of sellers of homogeneous product	
Under-provided by the market	

....

Q2: Explain the main causes of "market failure".

(15 marks)

....

Q3: Explain, using a diagram, how negative externalities can lead to the over consumption of a demerit good such as tobacco.

(15 marks)

Hint: The diagram will have two lines rising from left to right representing marginal social cost and marginal private cost. A line representing marginal benefit will fall from left to right.

....

Q4: Outline the main differences between the concept of perfect competition and the market circumstances that face a small hairdresser.

(15 marks)

....

Q5: Explain, with the help of diagrams, why monopoly can lead to the less efficient allocation of scarce resources.

(15 marks)

National and global economic issues

Unit 2 Topic 1

Recent trends in the national economy

Contents

Prerequisites

This topic assumes no previous knowledge and is intended to be accessible for those studying Economics for the first time. However, if you have already completed Higher Economics you will be familiar with some of the concepts outlined.

Learning objective

By the end of this topic you should be able to evaluate recent economic trends in the national economy by:

- describing recent trends in economic indicators;
- explaining reasons for a recent trend in an economic indicator;
- update all data with the latest information from respected sources.

This topic includes the latest economic trends at the time this note was produced. You will be asked to update these details and compose your own updated notes. Potential sources include the BBC, ONS, Guardian and Telegraph websites.

1.1 Gross domestic product (GDP)

The UK's economy grew by 2.6% in 2014. In 2013 the economy grew by 1.7%.

ONS figures showed the economy grew by 0.6% in the final three months of 2014, a slowdown from 0.7% growth recorded in the previous quarter.

The main points from the ONS report issued on 28 April 2015 are:

- Change in gross domestic product (GDP) is the main indicator of economic growth. GDP is estimated to have increased by 0.3% in Quarter 1 (Jan to Mar) 2015 compared with growth of 0.6% in Quarter 4 (Oct to Dec) 2014.
- Output increased in services by 0.5% in Quarter 1 2015. The other three main industrial groupings within the economy decreased, with construction falling by 1.6%, production by 0.1% and agriculture by 0.2%.
- GDP was 2.4% higher in Quarter 1 2015 compared with the same quarter a year ago.
- In Quarter 1 2015, GDP was estimated to have been 4.0% higher than the pre-economic downturn peak of Quarter 1 2008. From the peak in Quarter 1 2008 to the trough in Quarter 2 (Apr to June) 2009, the economy shrank by 6.0%.

Note that early ONS figures are prone to revision as more data comes in, although the changes are generally minor.

GDP Go online 

Q1: Locate the latest figures for the UK's gross domestic product and add them to your notes.

....

Q2: Locate two up-to-date articles, giving the main points regarding the recent progress of GDP. You may wish to retain these on a memory stick.

Suggested online sources: BBC, ONS, The Guardian, The Telegraph.

1.2 Inflation

Early in 2015, the rate of inflation turned negative (i.e. deflation), although both the Chancellor of the Exchequer and the Governor of the Bank of England stated that they did not expect this to continue for long.

In May 2015, the ONS drew attention to the following main points:

- The Consumer Prices Index (CPI) fell by 0.1% in the year to April 2015, compared to no change (0.0%) in the year to March 2015.
- This is the first time the CPI has fallen over the year since official records began in 1996 and the first time since 1960 based on comparable historic estimates.
- The largest downward contribution came from transport services - notably air and sea fares, with the timing of Easter this year a likely factor.

Inflation Go online

Q3: Locate the latest figures for the UK's inflation rate and add them to your notes.

....

Q4: Locate two up-to-date articles, giving the main points regarding the recent progress of inflation. You may wish to retain these on a memory stick.

Suggested online sources: BBC, ONS, The Guardian, The Telegraph.

1.3 Unemployment

In May 2015, the ONS drew attention to the following main points:

- Comparing the estimates for January to March 2015 with those for October to December 2014, employment continued to rise and unemployment continued to fall. These changes maintain the general direction of movement since late 2011 to early 2012.
- There were 31.1 million people in work, 202,000 more than for October to December 2014 and 564,000 more than for a year earlier.
- The proportion of people aged from 16 to 64 in work (the employment rate) was 73.5%, the highest since comparable records began in 1971.
- There were 1.83 million unemployed people. This was 35,000 fewer than for October to December 2014, the smallest quarterly fall since June to August 2013. Comparing January to March 2015 with a year earlier, there were 386,000 fewer unemployed people.
- The proportion of the economically active population who were unemployed (the unemployment rate) was 5.5%, lower than for October to December 2014 (5.7%) and for a year earlier (6.8%). The economically active population is those in work plus those seeking and available to work.

- There were 8.98 million people aged from 16 to 64 who were out of work and not seeking or available to work (known as **economically inactive**), 69,000 fewer than for October to December 2014 but little changed compared with a year earlier.
- The proportion of people aged from 16 to 64 who were economically inactive (the inactivity rate) was 22.1%, lower than for October to December 2014 (22.3%) but unchanged compared with a year earlier.
- Comparing January to March 2015 with a year earlier, pay for employees in Great Britain increased by 1.9% including bonuses and by 2.2% excluding bonuses.

A number of graphs sourced from the ONS are available, should you wish extra detail on employment trends.

Unemployment trends Go online 

Use your knowledge of economics and current affairs to comment on the possible reasons for the trends in each graph below. Discuss these with your teacher/tutor.

Q5: Jobless totals:

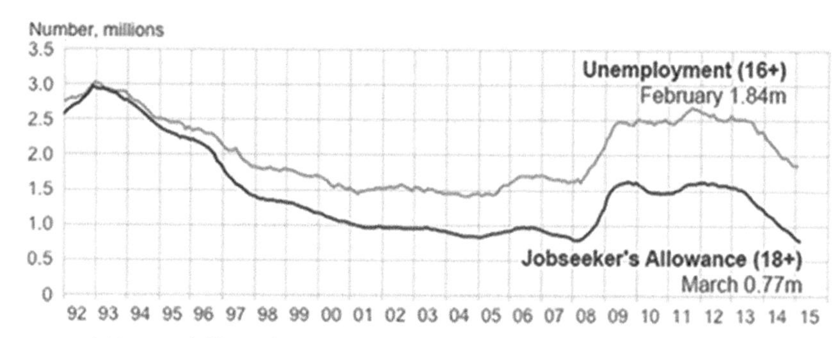

Jobless total: Unemployment and Jobseeker's Allowance in the UK 1992-2015
Source: ONS (Office of National Statistics)

....

Q6: Employment rates:

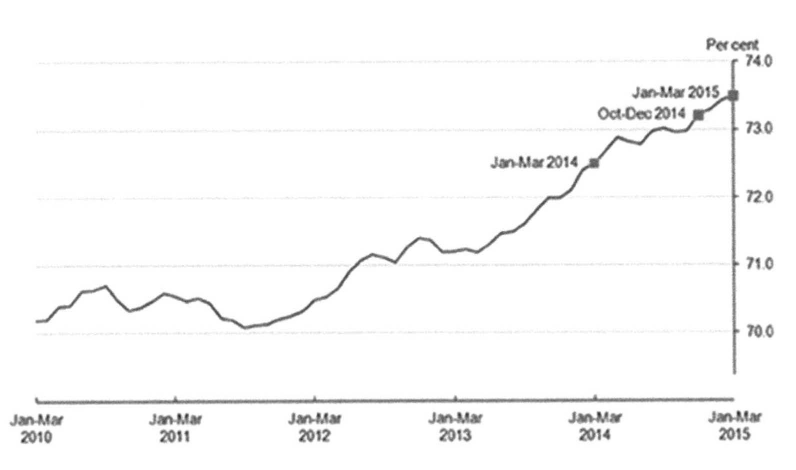

Employment rate (aged 16-64), **seasonally adjusted**
Source: ONS

. . . .

Q7: Public sector employment:

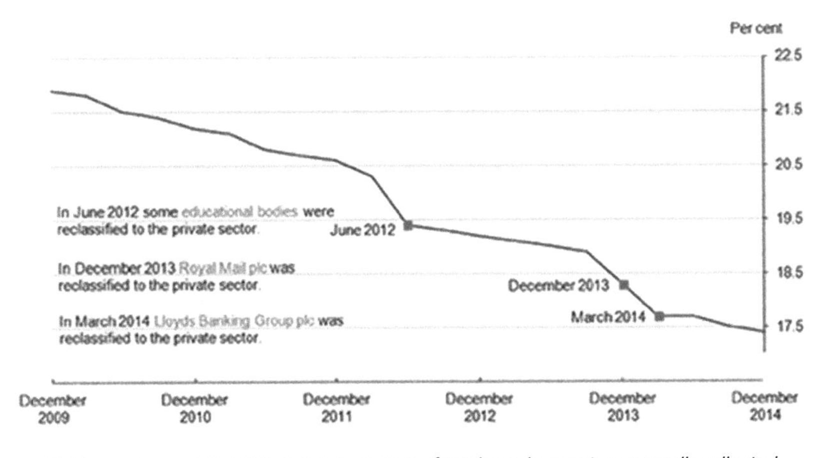

Public sector employment as a percentage of total employment, seasonally adjusted
Source: ONS

. . . .

Q8: Earnings and price growth:

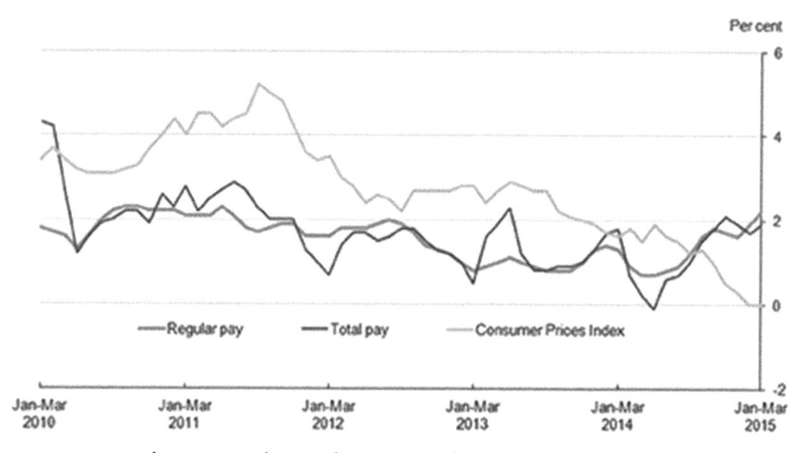

Average earnings and consumer prices annual growth rates
Source: ONS

....

Q9: Economic inactivity rate:

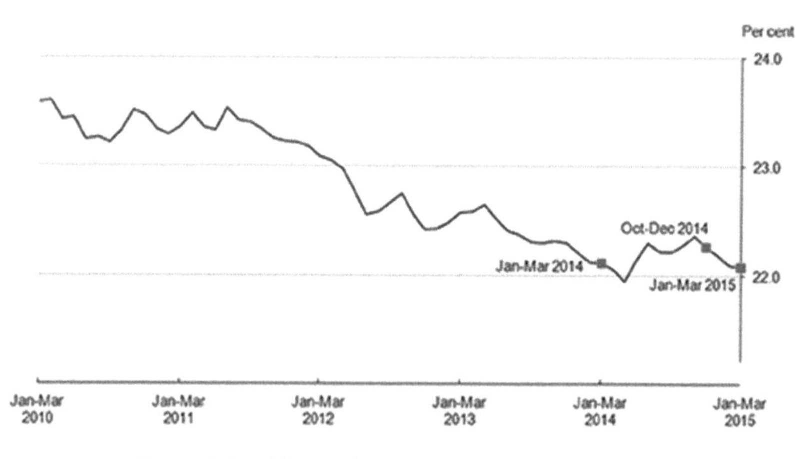

Economic inactivity rate (aged 16 to 64), seasonally adjusted
Source: ONS

Q10: Locate the latest figures for the UK's unemployment and add them to your notes.

....

Q11: Locate two up-to-date articles, giving the main points regarding the most recent changes in unemployment. You may wish to retain these on a memory stick.

Suggested online sources: BBC, ONS, The Guardian, The Telegraph.

1.4 The budget deficit

The deficit forecast to be 6.6% of GDP this year, 5.5% in 2014-15 then falling to 0.8% by 2017-18 with a surplus of 0.2% in 2018-19.

The government has not met their targets in this area in recent years, so it is likely that these forecasts will change.

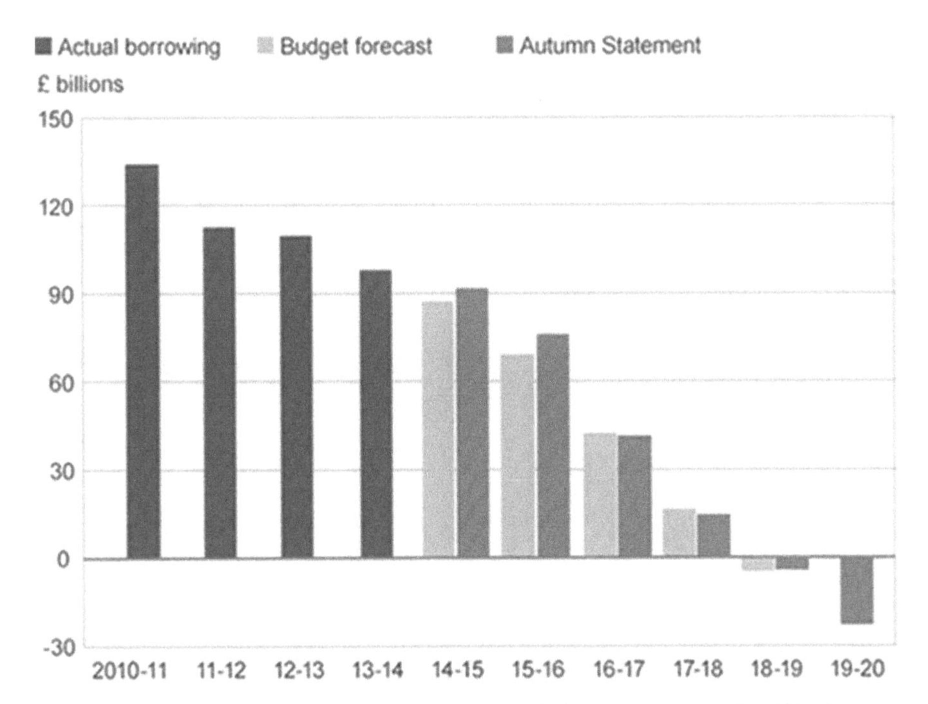

UK Government borrowing forecasts (excludes Royal Mail pension transfer, Asset Purchase Facility and public sector banks)
Source: ONS and OBR (Office for Budget Responsibility)

Borrowing was £108bn last year and is forecast to be under £90bn this year, leading to a surplus of almost £5bn in 2018-19.

The budget deficit Go online

Q12: How desirable is a balanced budget?

1.5 The exchange rate

The recent trend illustrated in the graphs below has been for the pound to weaken against the dollar, but to strengthen against the euro.

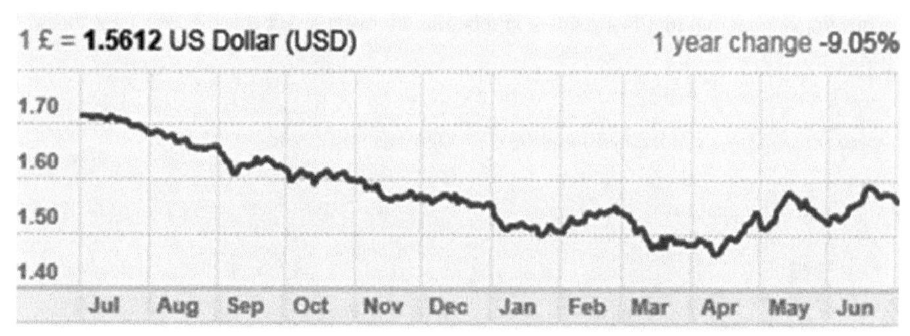

Exchange rate between UK pound sterling and US dollar
Source: The Financial Times (http://www.ft.com/markets)

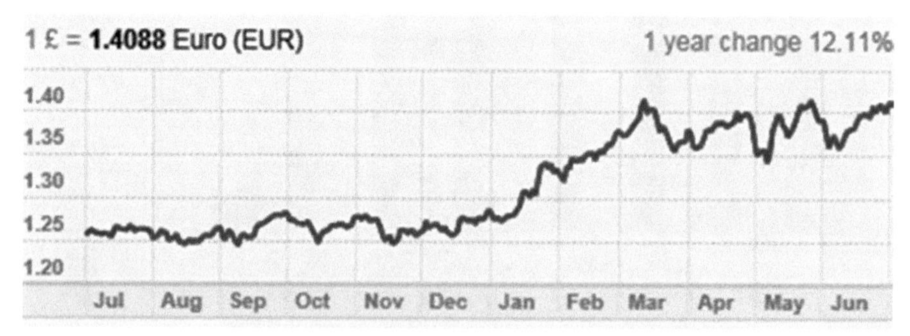

Exchange rate between UK pound sterling and the euro
Source: The Financial Times (http://www.ft.com/markets)

The exchange rate Go online 

Q13: Which of the three currencies has been strongest over the 12 months to May 2015?

....

Q14: Locate the latest figures for the exchange rate of the pound to both the dollar and the euro. Add them to your notes.

....

Q15: Locate two up-to-date articles, giving the main points regarding the most recent changes in exchange rates. You may wish to retain these on a memory stick.

Suggested online sources: BBC.

1.6 The balance of payments

ONS reported that:

- **Seasonally adjusted**, the UK's deficit on trade in goods and services was estimated to have been £2.8 billion in March 2015, compared with £3.3 billion in February 2015.
- This reflects a deficit of £10.1 billion on goods, partially offset by an estimated surplus of £7.3 billion on services.
- In Quarter 1 (Jan to Mar) 2015, the UK's deficit on trade in goods and services was estimated to have been £7.5 billion; widening by £1.5 billion from the previous quarter.
- In Quarter 1 2015, the trade in goods deficit widened by £0.8 billion to £29.9 billion. The widening reflects a £2.7 billion fall in exports and a £1.9 billion fall in imports.
- At the commodity level, the fall in exports in quarter 1 reflects a £2.2 billion decrease in exports of fuels; specifically, oil exported to EU countries, which fell by £2.1 billion from the previous quarter. Over the same period, imports of fuels fell by £2.2 billion, reflecting a £1.8 billion fall in imports of oil from outside the EU.

The balance of payments Go online 

Q16: Comment on the possible causes of fall in exports of goods from January to March.

Q17: Locate the latest figures for the UK's balance of payments and add them to your notes.

....

Q18: Locate two up-to-date articles, giving the main points regarding the most recent changes in the balance of payments. You may wish to retain these on a memory stick.

Suggested online sources: BBC, ONS, The Guardian, The Telegraph.

1.7 House prices

UK house prices accelerated with a 9.6% increase in the year to the end of March 2015, according to official figures.

A lack in the supply of homes on the market is thought to be behind the increase. The annual rate of increase accelerated from 7.4% a month earlier. In Scotland prices rose at 14.6%, the fastest since 2007. This was above the UK average.

The Land and Buildings Transaction Tax replaced UK stamp duty land tax in Scotland from 1 April, which "may have had an impact" on the increase in prices, according to the Office for National Statistics (ONS).

There were also double-digit percentage annual property price rises in the East of England (11.4%), London (11.2%) and the South East of England (11.2%), the ONS figures also show.

The ONS said that the cost of the average UK home in March was over £270,000, ranging from £498,000 in London to £145,000 in Northern Ireland (source: BBC website - http://bbc.in/1lih87g).

House prices Go online 

Q19: Locate the latest figures for the UK's house prices and add them to your notes.

....

Q20: Locate two up-to-date articles, giving the main points regarding the most recent changes in house prices. You may wish to retain these on a memory stick.

Suggested online sources: BBC, ONS, The Guardian, The Telegraph.

1.8 Oil prices

Oil comes in various types and qualities. As a benchmark for the prices of North Sea oil, that from the Brent field is typically quoted. The **spot market** is the price for immediate delivery, and can be slightly different from prices quoted on the **futures market** where contracts are for forward delivery. The diagram below shows that the spot price fell rapidly in late 2014.

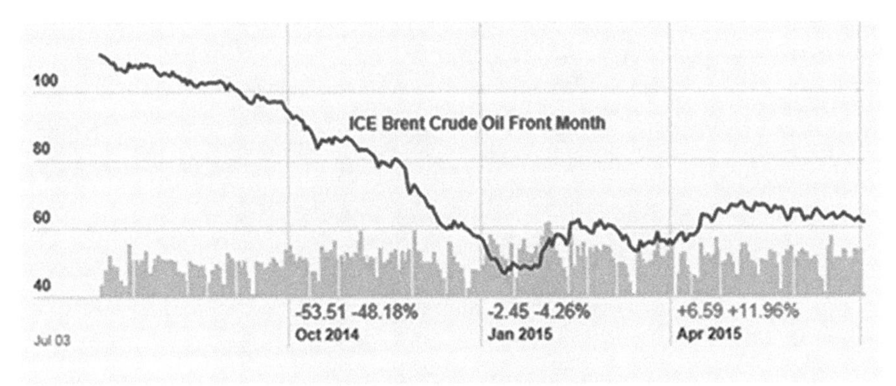

Brent crude oil spot price ($/barrel)
Source: The Financial Times (http://www.ft.com/markets)

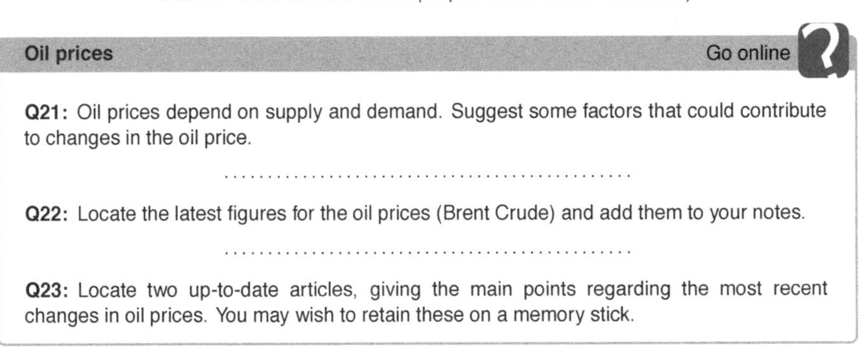

Oil prices Go online

Q21: Oil prices depend on supply and demand. Suggest some factors that could contribute to changes in the oil price.

....

Q22: Locate the latest figures for the oil prices (Brent Crude) and add them to your notes.

....

Q23: Locate two up-to-date articles, giving the main points regarding the most recent changes in oil prices. You may wish to retain these on a memory stick.

Suggested online sources: BBC, ONS, The Guardian, The Telegraph.

1.9 Summary

Summary

You should now be able to evaluate recent economic trends in the national economy by:

- describing recent trends in economic indicators;
- explaining reasons for a recent trend in an economic indicator;
- update all data with the latest information from respected sources.

Unit 2 Topic 2

Controlling the budget deficit and the national debt

Contents

Prerequisites

This topic assumes no previous knowledge and is intended to be accessible for those studying Economics for the first time. However if you have already completed Higher Economics you will be familiar with some of the concepts outlined.

Learning objective

By the end of this topic you should be able to:

- explain reasons why we have a budget deficit;
- explain the significance of the UK national debt;
- explain recent trends in the budget deficit;
- evaluate the effectiveness of recent government policy in reducing the budget deficit;
- update all data with the latest information from respected sources.

2.1 What makes this an important UK economic issue

One of the most significant issues affecting the UK economy is the size of the national debt, and the related issue of controlling the annual budget deficits which add to it. It has become a primary concern for UK governments and to date the attempts to reduce the deficit and the national debt have had mixed or even disappointing outcomes. It impacts on fiscal policy and through this on living standards and economic growth. This looks like continuing to be an issue for some years ahead.

This section illustrates some of the data and information that your research should reveal. If you are considering a dissertation in this area, you will need to update all the data that follows. Therefore, the major activity to be carried out throughout this topic is to obtain the latest figures.

2.2 Why the UK has a budget deficit

The UK has a budget deficit for the following reasons:

- ***Fiscal policy*** - the UK Government in the majority of years has public spending levels that exceed its tax revenues;
- ***The structural deficit*** - the UK Government makes major infrastructure investments which, although beneficial to the economy in the long term, add to the borrowing requirement. This **structural deficit** continues even when the economy is expanding;
- ***Recession*** - during recessions, UK Government spending in areas such as welfare increases but at the same time tax revenues reduce because personal and corporate incomes fall;
- ***Interest payments*** - maintaining the debt requires the payment of interest every year and this places further pressure on government spending. Higher bond yields will cause interest payments to increase.

Budget deficit reasons Go online 

Match the reason for a budget deficit with the statements in the following questions.

Q1: A decline in economic activity reduces tax revenues.

a) Fiscal policy
b) The structural deficit
c) Recession
d) Interest payments

....

Q2: Borrowing for major infrastructure investment.

a) Fiscal policy
b) The structural deficit
c) Recession
d) Interest payments

....

Q3: Government spends more than it raises.

a) Fiscal policy
b) The structural deficit
c) Recession
d) Interest payments

....

Q4: The cost of funding the national debt curbs spending.

a) Fiscal policy
b) The structural deficit
c) Recession
d) Interest payments

2.2.1 Why 2009/10 was the peak year for borrowing

Public sector borrowing peaked in 2009/10 at £167.4bn. Factors that contributed to this exceptional year included:

- the economic crisis that followed the "credit crunch" resulted in reduced incomes and hence reduced income tax receipts;
- a cut in the rate of VAT which was a fiscal measure aimed at increasing aggregate demand and stimulating the economy but in the short term reduced tax revenues.
- higher benefits were paid due to higher unemployment in recession;
- Government spending on areas such as the NHS had increased significantly over the decade.

Government borrowing Go online 

Q5: Why does government have to borrow?

2.2.2 The issue of asset sales from the public sector

Note that the government can make asset sales from the public sector and this is regarded as reducing the annual deficit. Therefore the privatisation of Royal Mail contributed to a reduction in that year's deficit. Funds from the sale of the assets are further increased by the receipt of the Royal Mail pension fund.

The government had to adopt the pension fund liabilities of the Royal Mail to make the sale attractive to the private investors. These pension fund liabilities will run forward for decades and add to public spending and hence the deficit. In other words, an apparent reduction in one year's deficit could turn out to have a negative impact on the deficit overall in the long term.

Sale of public sector assets Go online 

Q6: What is questionable about treating the sale of public sector assets as income for one year?

2.3 The extent of UK national debt and how it compares with other countries

The national debt is the accumulation of government borrowing over centuries. Every year in which there is a budget deficit adds to it. The government has to pay interest on this debt to finance it and this varies with interest rates but typically will be tens of billions of pounds. In order to reduce the national debt the government would need to have a budget surplus.

It should also be recognised that the UK national debt:

- is currently financed at low rates of interest;
- has repayment dates that are more spread out over the medium and long term than those of many other countries;
- is to an extent owed to others within the UK economy such as pension funds and individuals (and this portion is a transfer of income from taxpayers to savers and does not leave the UK economy).

In 2015, the government considers control of the budget deficit as an economic priority. The chancellor (George Osborne) announced that the Committee of the Commissioners for the Reduction of the National Debt would meet for the first time in more than 150 years. This group which includes the governor of the Bank of England last met in the aftermath of the Napoleonic Wars to address the issue of national debt.

The following map shows a comparison of the gross debt of the 28 European Union member states as a percentage of GDP (figures from 2013).

The absolute value of the national debt is not helpful for international or historic comparisons. Everything is relative, and for this topic the key measure is the national debt compared to annual GDP. This shows the significance of the debt by comparing it to the overall annual output of a nation's economy. The map below follows and illustrates this point.

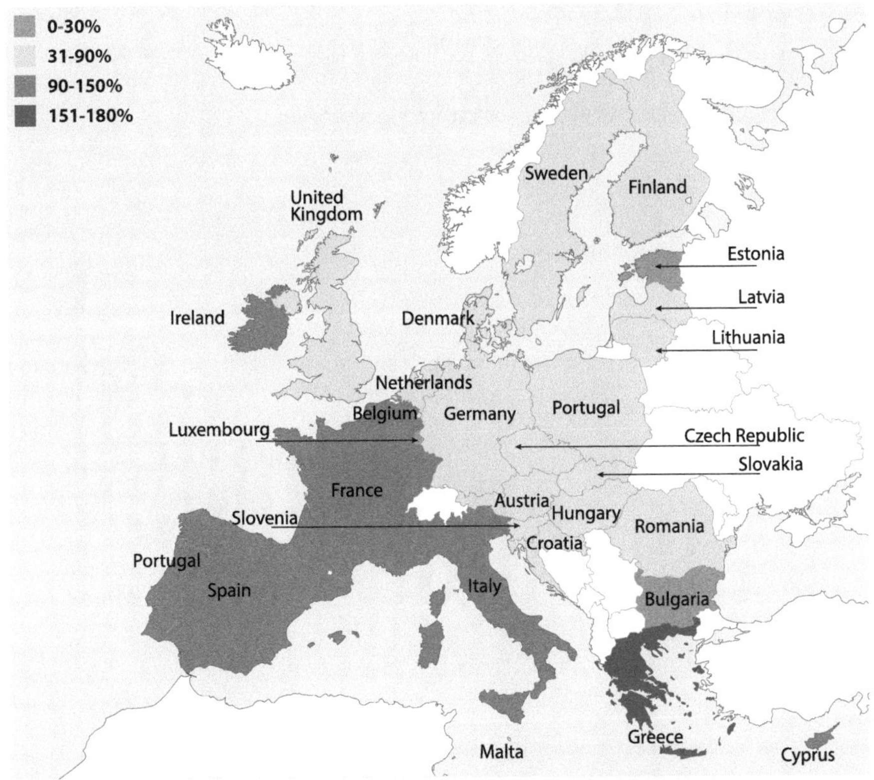

Gross debt of European Union member states as a percentage of GDP

National debt comparison Go online 

Q7: Name the European Union member countries that have a greater problem with their accumulated national debt than the UK.

The column chart that follows will help you to confirm your answer.

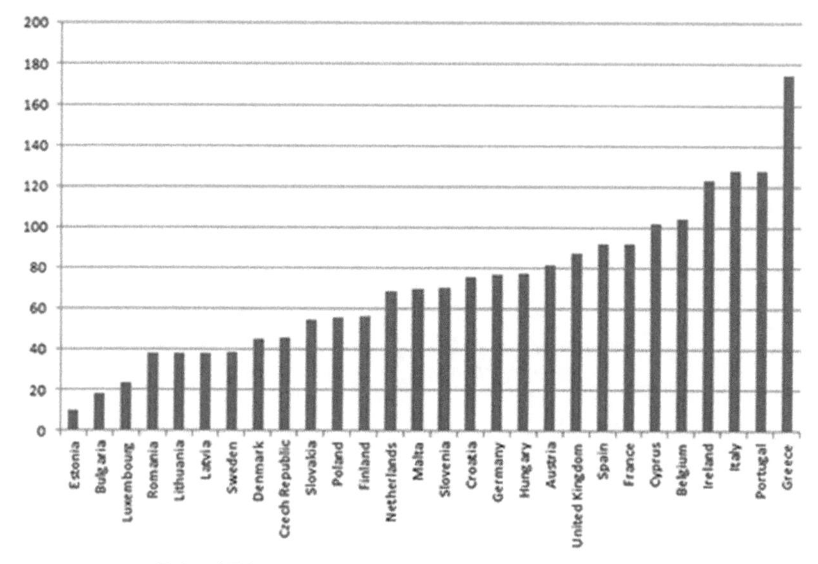

Debt of EU countries as a percentage of GDP (end of 2013)

....

Q8: Carry out some research and establish the debt to GDP ratios of:

a) USA;
b) Japan;
c) Australia.

....

Q9: Research the most recent figures available for the debt of EU countries.

....

Q10: Find a UK national debt calculator online. You could note down the current figure, but it will change as you look at it! You may also find a calculator for the US debt.

2.4 How the current UK deficit compares with historic levels

The diagram below shows net UK Government borrowing and indicates the dramatic increase in the UK deficit in recent years.

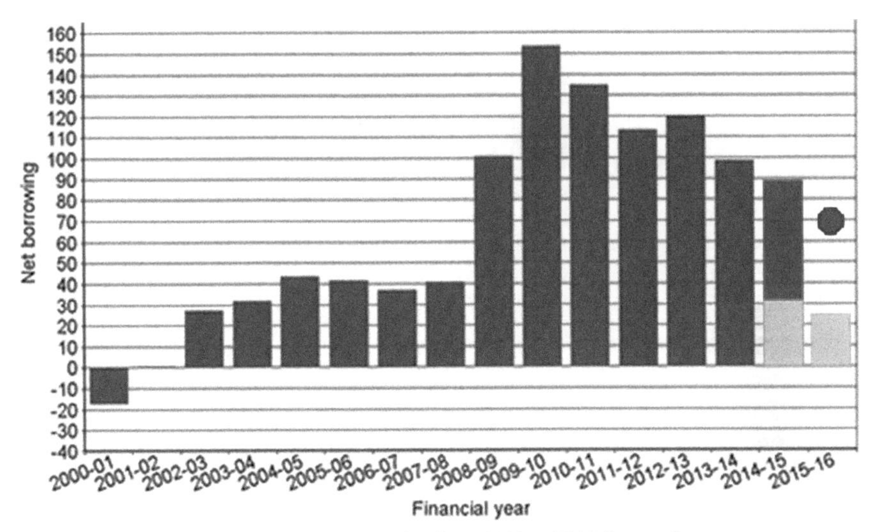

UK public sector borrowing from 2001 to 2016 (forecast)
(Source: ONS (http://bit.ly/1FjSLpd))

Net borrowing year to date for 2014-15 and 2015-16 is shown in light blue. The dark blue dot indicates the full financial year forecast for 2015-16.

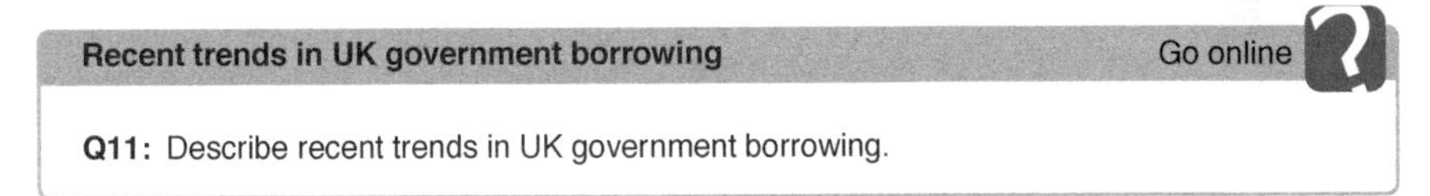
Recent trends in UK government borrowing Go online

Q11: Describe recent trends in UK government borrowing.

The comparison of UK net borrowing to the GDP is a useful way of looking at the relative size of the budget deficit. The years ahead are forecasts and going on the failure of previous predictions, may not turn out as expected.

The bar graph below shows the UK net borrowing as a percentage of GDP using figures from the Office of National Statistics. The bars showing light blue denote the forecast figures (future predictions).

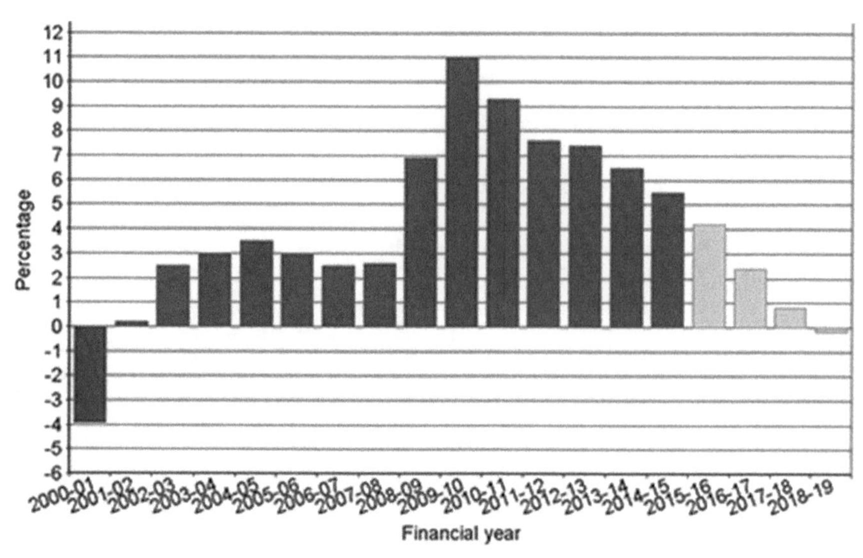

UK net borrowing as a percentage of GDP

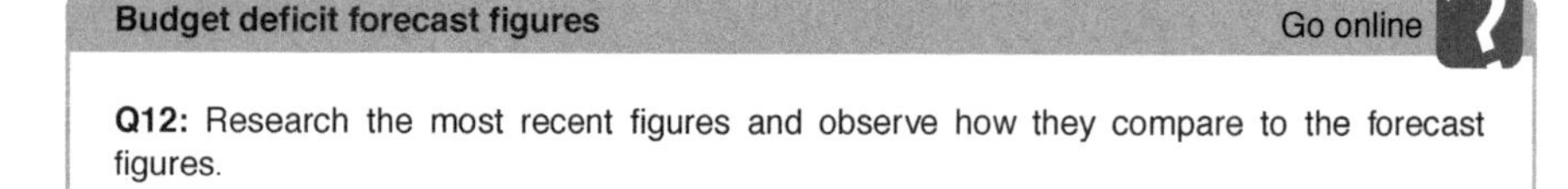

Budget deficit forecast figures Go online

Q12: Research the most recent figures and observe how they compare to the forecast figures.

2.5 The effectiveness of recent government policy in reducing the budget deficit

The latest figures available, at the time of writing, show that **public sector net borrowing (PSNB)** was £86.3bn from April to December 2014. This is only 0.1% lower than the same period in 2013. During the same period the national debt increased significantly.

The newly elected government of 2015 has put forward the following proposal on the topic of budget deficits.

The Chancellor of the Exchequer, George Osborne, said,

> "In normal times, governments of the left as well as the right should run a budget surplus to bear down on debt and prepare for an uncertain future".

This is a pledge to balance the public sector books but of course it remains at the whim of a future government to change this approach.

Given how tightly public spending has already been squeezed over the years 2010-2015, it will be very difficult and probably not desirable to reduce it as rapidly as the Chancellor has indicated. The level of debt has continued to increase despite the reductions in public spending and many view the policy of austerity as having failed (see article below).

As a student of Economics you should research and form your own view on the efficacy of the government policy. The opposition statements below should not be treated uncritically.

The extract below is from the Sunday Herald (5 July 2015) where the SNP's John Swinney presents the opinion under the headline 'The cuts don't work... stop them'.

> "The experiment in austerity has been a failure by any benchmark. GDP per capita - a key measure of our economic strength - is forecast to take two years longer to return to pre-recession levels than it did following the Great Depression of the 1930s.
>
> Austerity has even failed in its principal objective of cutting the deficit. Over the six years to 2016, the Chancellor is likely to miss the borrowing targets he set for himself when he first entered office in 2010 by a staggering £150 billion. It's simple economics that a programme of austerity and cuts that reduces household income and damages economic confidence weakens rather than strengthens the public finances."

The Labour Party's spokesperson said,

> "The figures show George Osborne has broken his promise to balance the books by this year and national debt is still rising."
>
> "His failure on the deficit is because falling living standards over the last five years have led to tax revenues falling short. This government is now set to have borrowed over £200bn more than planned."

Reliability of sources Go online 

Q13: Consider the reliability of the opposition sources quoted above.

2.6 Summary

Summary

You should now be able to:

- explain reasons why we have a budget deficit;
- explain the significance of the UK national debt;
- explain recent trends in the budget deficit;
- evaluate the effectiveness of recent government policy in reducing the budget deficit;
- update all data with the latest information from respected sources.

2.7 End of topic test

End of Topic 2 test Go online 

Q14: Which of these does ***not*** cause the annual budget deficit to increase?

a) Higher interest charges on the national debt
b) Higher rates of economic growth
c) Increased infrastructure spending by government
d) Reductions in VAT receipts

....

Q15: UK net borrowing as a percent of GDP peaked in:

a) 2008-09
b) 2009-10
c) 2010-11
d) 2011-12

....

Q16: The structural deficit exists because of:

a) increased benefit spending during recession.
b) reduced income tax receipts during recession.
c) long-term investment in infrastructure by government.
d) the privatisation of public sector assets.

....

Q17: Government policies from 2010-1015 that have been described as "austerity" have by the end of that period:

a) led to a reduction in the national debt.
b) produced a shorter downturn than the great depression of the 1930s.
c) have left the UK with one of the smallest borrowing to GDP percentages in the EU.
d) led to falls in UK net borrowing as a percentage of GDP.

Unit 2 Topic 3

Trends in the Scottish oil industry

Contents

Prerequisites

This topic assumes no previous knowledge and is intended to be accessible for those studying Economics for the first time. However if you have already completed Higher Economics you will be familiar with some of the concepts outlined.

Learning objective

By the end of this topic you should be able to:

- describe recent economic trends in the oil industry;
- explain oil price fluctuations;
- evaluate the impact of oil price changes on the Scottish economy;
- update all data with the latest information from respected sources.

3.1 Production trends in the North Sea oil industry

This topic examines the latest economic trends in the oil industry at the time of publishing. You will be asked to update these details and compose your own updated notes. This will provide you with the latest information.

Your main sources could be the BBC and ONS websites. Alternatively you may search for alternative articles - The Guardian and The Telegraph websites are two possible sources of relevant articles. The Aberdeen-based regional daily The Press and Journal will also contain many oil-related articles.

Some of these newspaper articles are written against the background of Scottish politics and contain a significant political bias so should be handled with care.

3.2 Falling UK oil production

Using the expected boundary line in the North Sea between Scotland and the rest of the UK, more than 95% of oil production would have been in the Scottish sector in recent years. (50-60% of current UK gas production is also produced in the Scottish sector.)

Exploration effort has decreased but demand for licenses is high.

Interest in the North Sea remains high with 410 blocks licensed in the 27th round. This is an all-time high.

Licensing round Go online 

Q1: The figure for the 28th licensing round was published in the week this topic was prepared. Find out how many blocks were awarded in this round and any subsequent licensing rounds. Read any accompanying article(s).

Production to present: 42 billion barrels.

Remaining North Sea oil has been estimated to be in the range of 15-24 billion barrels. (Source: Oil and Gas UK)

The Department of Energy & Climate Change (DECC) estimate predicts 11-21 billion barrels. The DECC has also produced a very cautious prediction of 10.4 billion barrels produced by 2050.

Reliability of sources Go online 

Q2: Consider the reliability of the following sources (referred to above):

a) Oil and Gas UK;
b) The Department of Energy and Climate Change.

Here is a summary taken from a report on the BBC website dated 28 July 2015 that refers to the quarterly output in the oil and gas sector.

> "UK economic growth accelerated in the second quarter of the year, helped by a big jump in oil and gas production, official figures have shown.
>
> The ONS said manufacturing output experienced its first fall in two years with output dropping 0.3% in the quarter. However, a surge in North Sea oil and gas production lifted overall industrial output by 1% - the biggest increase since late 2010. The "mining and quarrying" component of the industrial output figures, which includes oil and gas extraction, rose by 7.8% in the quarter, the biggest increase since 1989.
>
> The ONS said the increase, which came despite falling oil prices, was driven by tax cuts in March designed to support the sector."

Quarterly output in the oil and gas sector Go online 

Q3: Locate this article and an up-to-date equivalent. With these quarterly figures being regularly announced by the ONS, the information will be available on a range of news, business or economics websites. How has the situation altered since 2015?

3.3 Oil price trends and predictions

As with predicted production, there are different views on the direction of future oil prices in the medium term.

The Office of Budget Responsibility (OBR) predict that prices will fall. The International Energy Agency, Department of Energy and Climate Change and US Department of Energy believe that prices will rise.

Given this divergence of opinion among specialised agencies, you with your knowledge of Economics, should feel capable of making your own mind up - either way, you won't be without support.

Oil price predictions may influence the UK constitutional debate on Scotland. This is because oil revenues would be a significant contribution to the GDP and public finances of an independent Scotland.

The diagram below shows the price of Brent Crude (the North Sea benchmark for oil prices) on the first of every month since 1 September 2013 in US dollars.

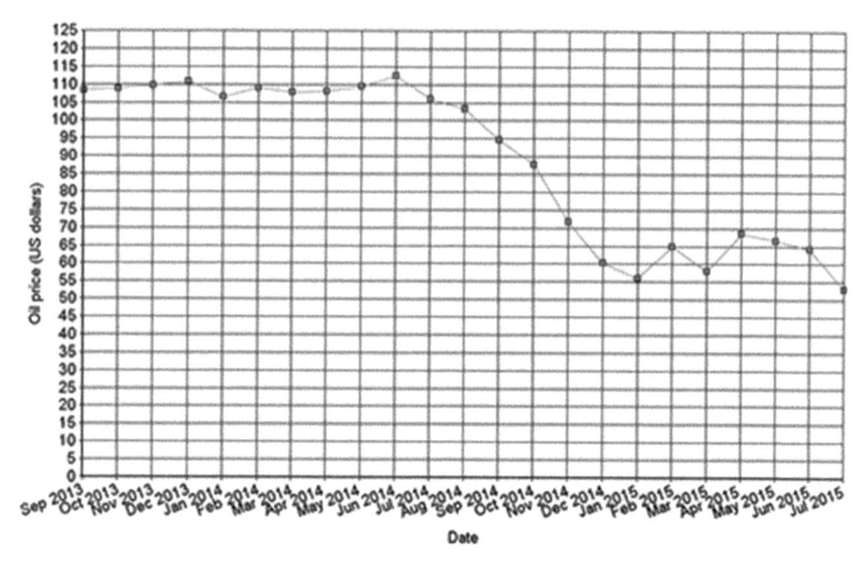

Brent Crude oil prices (in US dollars) from 2013 to 2015

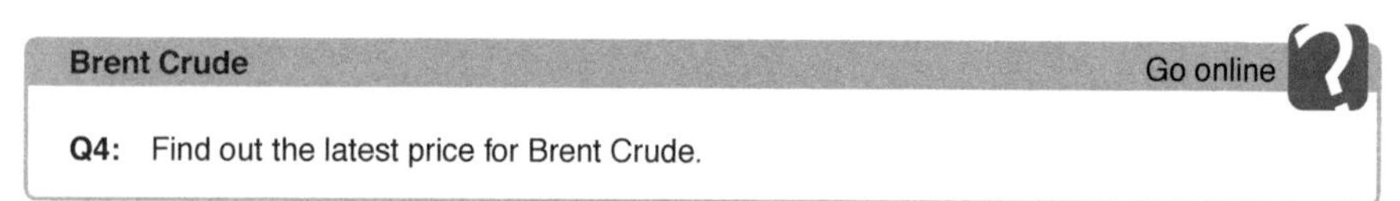

Brent Crude Go online

Q4: Find out the latest price for Brent Crude.

3.4 Causes of oil price fluctuations

Oil prices fluctuate in a global market and as with any market, the interaction of supply and demand causes the price to move.

In June 2014, the price of Brent crude was up around $115 per barrel which highlights the significant drop in prices, so why have they fallen?

Demand factors

Demand for energy is closely related to economic activity. For the majority of the past decade, oil prices have been high, often above $100 per barrel. Soaring oil consumption in countries like China meant that oil production in conventional fields couldn't keep up with demand, so prices rose.

From Autumn 2014, demand for oil in places like Europe, Asia, and the USA began tapering off, due to weakening economies and new efficiency measures.

Demand is low because of lower economic growth in China, continuing problems in the Eurozone, increased efficiency, and a growing switch away from oil to other fuels. For example, vehicles are becoming more energy-efficient. Even the seasons and the weather play a part as demand increases in the winter in the northern hemisphere.

Supply factors

High prices had encouraged companies in the USA and Canada to start drilling for new, hard-to-extract crude in North Dakota's shale formations and Alberta's oil sands. By the end of 2014, world oil supply was on track to rise beyond actual demand, so the unused oil was simply stored for later. Storage space is limited and so purchases of oil (demand) fell, causing a decrease in prices.

Supply can also be affected by weather such as hurricanes in the Gulf of Mexico, and by political instability in oil-producing regions such as Iraq and Libya. Price expectations have an important effect. If producers think the price is staying high, they invest, which after a lag boosts supply. Similarly, low prices lead to an investment drought.

The USA has become the world's largest oil producer. Though it does not export crude oil, it now imports much less, creating a lot of spare supply. United States domestic production has nearly doubled over the six years to 2014.

The market is far from perfect and, although the **OPEC** cartel has less influence on prices, the biggest players remain Saudi Arabia and their Gulf allies. They have decided not to sacrifice their own market share. Saudi officials have said that if they cut production and prices go up, they will lose market share and merely benefit their competitors. The Saudis expect other producers to fill the gap if they reduce production.

In 2014 OPEC failed to reach agreement on production curbs, sending the price tumbling.

Market factors Go online 

Q5: Put the following market factors into the correct column in the table below:

- Cold winter in the northern hemisphere;
- Increasing miles per gallon of modern cars;
- Libya described as a "failed state";
- Reduced economic growth in China;
- Soaring shale oil production in USA.

Supply	Demand

3.5 The impact of oil prices on the Scottish economy

Tax revenues from oil and gas have overwhelmingly come from the Scottish sector (85-94% in recent years). Relative to the tax base of Scotland, these would be large and volatile revenues, but in the context of the UK these revenues are less significant. Declines in production and larger capital allowances have recently reduced tax revenues.

The OBR projects falling tax revenues as it predicts relatively low prices and production. The Scottish Government is more optimistic and expects a revival of these revenues based on higher prices and increased production. Changes in oil prices, production levels and capital allowances all have an impact on the oil-related activities which concentrate around centres such as Aberdeen and Shetland.

It is worth considering whether the overall impact of lower oil prices on the economy of the UK (and perhaps to a lesser extent, Scotland) will be advantageous.

Here are a few points to consider:

- Falling petrol prices left consumers with additional income to dispose of in other ways. This expenditure may have contributed to the increase in economic growth in late 2014 / early 2015 (which was convenient for a government heading into an election).
- Economic growth is good for employment.
- The reduced inflation stemming from falling petrol prices would increase real incomes.
- Reduced inflation will also delay a rise in interest rates, assisting borrowers and investors.
- Productivity in the North Sea may increase as a result of cost-cutting economies and this may further extend the life of many fields.

Many jobs have been lost in the oil sector of the economy, and you should consider this through the following two activities.

North Sea job loss announcements Go online 

Q6: Online find at least two examples of job loss announcements related to the North Sea during 2015.

....

Q7: Consider the multiplier effect arising from these job losses.

3.6 Summary

Summary

You should now be able to:

- describe recent economic trends in the oil industry;
- explain oil price fluctuations;
- evaluate the impact of oil price changes on the Scottish economy;
- update all data with the latest information from respected sources.

3.7 End of topic test

End of Topic 3 test Go online

Q8: During most of 2014 oil prices were often:

a) above $120.
b) between $100 and $120.
c) between $60 and $100.
d) below $60.

....

Q9: Using the expected boundary line in the North Sea between Scotland and the rest of the UK, the proportion of oil production that takes place in the Scottish section of the North Sea in recent years is:

a) between 50% and 60%.
b) between 60% and 75%.
c) between 75% and 90%.
d) over 90%.

....

Q10: The demand for oil depends on:

a) the weather in oil-producing regions.
b) political stability in oil-producing nations.
c) economic growth around the world.
d) changes in capital allowances that reduce taxes on oil.

....

Q11: The supply of oil depends on:

a) new technology for developing shale oil.
b) the reduced fuel consumption of modern vehicles.
c) energy conservation measures.
d) economic growth in China.

....

Q12: Lower oil prices could benefit the UK economy by:

i. reducing inflationary pressure.
ii. increasing consumption in other areas of the economy.
iii. improving productivity in the North Sea.

a) i) and ii) only
b) i) and iii) only
c) ii) and iii) only
d) all of the above

Unit 2 Topic 4

Global economic issues: globalisation

Contents

Prerequisites

This topic assumes no previous knowledge and is intended to be accessible for those studying Economics for the first time. However, if you have already completed Higher Economics you will be familiar with some of the concepts outlined.

Learning objective

By the end of this topic you should be able to:

- explain the concept of globalisation;
- analyse the benefits of globalisation and the problems it may bring;
- analyse the reasons (including globalisation) for the rapid economic growth of China;
- research effectively a wide range of economic data.

4.1 Introduction

The twin catalysts for the recent surge in **globalisation** appear to have been the revolution in information and communication technologies combined with the rampant and universal capitalism that has followed the acceptance of markets by the formerly centrally planned socialist economies such as Russia and China.

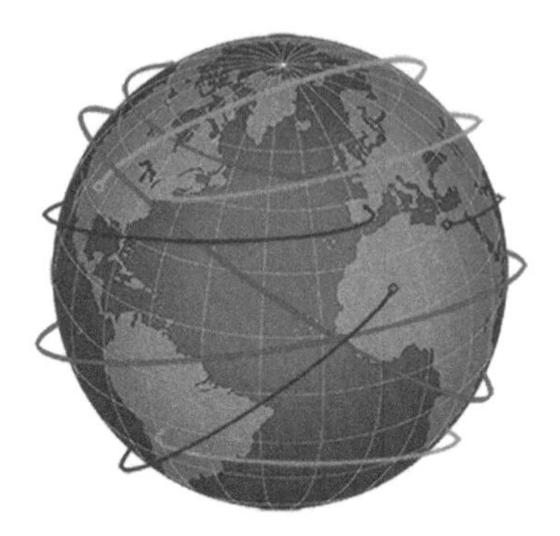

Global trade routes

The world's economies have developed ever-closer links in the process known as globalisation. China and India have made big steps forward and by their sheer size are prominent in the process, but among smaller countries such as Taiwan and Vietnam, globalisation continues apace. Taiwan is an excellent example of an open market economy that began to thrive in the 1960s, and seems to have embraced the concept of globalisation even before the term had been coined. The deregulation of markets, the development of free trade in goods and capital markets, and improvements in transport and communications have generated a vast increase in prosperity in some previously poor countries.

Globalisation Go online 

Watch a short video on YouTube entitled 'Did you know 3.0?' (https://youtu.be/YmwwrGV_aiE) giving a flavour of globalisation (video last updated 2012).

4.2 Definitions of globalisation

Globalisation has many definitions. Collins dictionary suggests globalisation is the "process enabling financial and investment markets to operate internationally, largely as a result of **deregulation** and improved communications".

The United Nations body, ESCWA (Economic and Social Commission for Western Asia), states globalisation "when used in an economic context refers to the reduction and removal of barriers between national borders in order to facilitate the flow of goods, capital, services and labour... although considerable barriers remain to the flow of labour."

Globalisation has been compared to living in a world without frontiers. Increases in international trade, communications and investment have been the driving forces behind further economic integration, and the increasingly free movement of goods, capital and then people and culture in a global marketplace.

Critics denounce globalisation as leading to a world economy dominated by multinational companies that cannot be regulated by national governments.

Globalisation definition Go online 

Read the entry for globalisation on Wikipedia (http://bit.ly/1Uy5VuX).

Q1: What were the four basic aspects of globalisation identified by the IMF?

4.3 The effects of globalisation

Here are a number of economic examples of extending globalisation:

- **Multinational** companies have always been in the vanguard of globalisation, for example Ford in the USA and BP in the UK. Now the process has accelerated, expanded, and is inclusive of newly industrialised countries so that examples include Tata of India owning the UK's Jaguar brand.
- Global brand recognition was once the territory of a few iconic brands such as Ford or Coca Cola which, for many years, would have been largely unrecognised in China, the world's most populated nation. Now the list of global brands extends, and the opening of formerly planned economies to markets and private enterprise has made them truly global.
- In the car industry, components are sourced from around the globe. Throughout business, globalisation has seen a willingness to source parts and products from around the world, and the cost savings are passed on to the consumer as competitive prices. Firms choose low cost locations around the globe, or outsource services such as call centre work, to India, for example.
- Another feature is the emergence of more free trade areas in the style of the EU and the extension into common standards and the free movement of labour. The clichéd example in the UK is the Polish plumber.

Worldwide financial markets have developed and regulators have still to internationalise, catch up and impose authority.

The growth of English as the international language of business continues and the vast majority of internet traffic occurs in English. China will shortly be the nation with the greatest number of English speakers.

Tata group Go online 

Q2: Find out which countries the Tata group operate in and identify some of the products they produce.

4.4 Analysis of the advantages of globalisation

Ten of the claimed advantages of globalisation are listed below:

1. ***Improvements in standards of living***

   There is plenty of evidence to show that countries that have embraced capitalism and free markets and have enjoyed large-scale foreign direct investment have prospered. Examples from recent history include Taiwan, Brazil and Singapore. One claim is that three billion people have been lifted from poverty in the last 50 years alongside increasing globalisation.

2. ***Improvements in life expectancy***

   With economic growth comes the tax base that enables government to make wholesale improvements to sanitation, drinking water supplies and health care leading to greater **life expectancy**. Government may have used foreign aid to make initial progress, and this can be the start of the virtuous cycle of economic growth and investment in public welfare. One figure quoted is that 85% of the world's population now live to at least 60 years old. This represents a rapid improvement in the outlook for many people who previously lived in abject poverty.

3. ***Improvements in literacy rates***

   Spending on basic education and improving **literacy rates** is vital if a poor country is to achieve economic take-off. When government has no funds and little to tax this is a difficult process to initiate. Foreign aid will play a major part, but if a country encourages entrepreneurship and is open to foreign investment then new funds do become available to families and to government that can be invested in the education of the next generation. It can be argued that globalisation speeds up this process.

4. ***Dramatic reductions in costs of production***

   Globalisation reaps the benefits of the trade theory of comparative advantage writ large. Goods and services can be produced in the most efficient, lowest cost locations, where the four factors of production plus transport costs to market are minimised. Modern communications allow UK call centres to operate in India and for multinational firms to manufacture in Vietnam. The result is that costs and prices are contained and reduced, increasing standards of living globally.

5. ***The spread of new technology***

   Modern technology reaches less developed countries rapidly. The term "intermediate technology" was in use to describe the need to supply poorer countries with technology that was basic and could be operated and repaired by local people. Globalisation, it could be argued, enables countries to pass quickly through this halfway house stage in economic development. Modern communications and improvements in literacy and education allow up-to-date technology to reach open economies. Multinational firms bring with them multinational advanced technologies.

6. ***Improved environmental performance***

   When people are poor and starving, there is little funding to deal with environmental issues. As economic growth increases, so does the possibility of diverting some of this increased income into protecting the environment. Modern technologies are often less polluting technologies. Increased environmental awareness is a feature of globalisation.

7. ***Improvements in working conditions***

   Companies moving to developing countries bring jobs, higher wages and usually better working conditions compared with domestic companies. Wages are lower in developing countries than those in advanced economies, but experience in countries like Taiwan shows that as countries develop economically wages improve and the "sweat shops" and labour intensive industries change to more capital intensive and knowledge-based industries. Multinationals generally bring working conditions and workplace standards that are higher than those provided by local firms and they pay more.

8. ***Greater knowledge of and respect for other cultures***

   Higher levels of migration increases the awareness and, generally, the tolerance of other cultures.

9. ***Extension of democracy***

   The gradual improvement in human rights and the development of democratic systems of government have generally progressed alongside globalisation.

10. ***Increased international cooperation***

    The level of interdependence in the world economy has strengthened institutions such as the World Trade Organisation and the World Bank. Governments have cooperated to establish international rules for the conduct of the global economy.

Benefits of globalisation - video Go online 

Q3: Watch the documentary 'Globalisation is Good - Johan Norberg on Globalisation' (https://youtu.be/12YDLZq8rT4) available on YouTube, courtesy of Channel 4. As you watch, summarise the main themes.

You can compare your summary with the themes noted in the answer.

Benefits of globalisation Go online 

Q4: Select the appropriate missing words and phrases from the following list to complete the list of the benefits of globalisation below:

- conditions;
- costs of production;
- cultures;
- democracy;
- environmental;
- international;
- life;
- literacy;
- living;
- technology.

Benefits of globalisation:

1. Improvements in standards of ....
2. Improvements in .... expectancy
3. Improvements in .... rates
4. Dramatic reductions in ....
5. The spread of new ....
6. Improved .... performance
7. Improvements in working ....
8. Greater knowledge of and respect for other ....
9. Extension of ....
10. Increased .... cooperation

4.4.1 Case studies - advantages of globalisation

Life expectancy Go online 

Q5: Using the CIA World Factbook (http://1.usa.gov/1FY6ErF), find the life expectancy in the following sample countries:

a) UK, Japan and Canada - advanced economies;
b) Singapore, Taiwan and Brazil - early gainers from globalisation;
c) Vietnam - recent gainers from globalisation;
d) Kenya - where globalisation has been restrained by government policy.

Literacy rates

Q6: Using the CIA World Factbook (http://1.usa.gov/1FY6ErF) , find the literacy rates in the following sample countries:

a) Singapore, Taiwan and Brazil;

b) Vietnam;

c) Kenya.

Effect of globalisation on the Taiwan, Brazil and Singapore economies Go online

Q7: Research the economies of Taiwan, Brazil and Singapore online to backup the assertion that globalisation has improved these countries' standards of living.

4.5 Analysis of the disadvantages of globalisation

Ten of the claimed disadvantages of globalisation are listed below:

1. ***Problems associated with the restructuring of economies***

   In the short term, countries will lose uncompetitive industries as they are opened up to international competition. This will cause painful economic readjustments and higher unemployment in the short term.

2. ***Widening gap between richest and poorest countries***

   In 1960, the top richest fifth of countries in the world were 30 times richer than the poorest fifth. This gap had risen to 85 times richer by 1995. Globalisation as a process has thrown up winners among those countries that can adapt, but those nations that lack the basic infrastructure to attract foreign investment have failed to progress. Advanced economies have certainly done well out of globalisation, but further down the pecking order the outcomes are more mixed.

3. ***Destruction of traditional agricultural communities***

   A traditional way of rural life can vanish forever and local customs and culture may fade. Urbanisation does come with rising living standards and people are tempted away by the promise of prosperity. This is possibly bad news for tourists and social anthropologists, but generally considered progress by those that are no longer dependent on a good harvest in order to eat.

4. ***Movement of skilled workers to the richest countries***

   As the migration of labour is freed up and gathers pace, so some countries lose skilled workers to advanced economies that pay better. However, many return home with capital and ideas. Many send money home to family.

5. ***Easier spread of disease***

   One example of this arises from the tobacco industry. Markets in advanced economies began to shrink in the face of adverse publicity regarding the health problems associated with smoking. Multinational companies stand accused of profiting by expanding into countries where government regulation was minimal and anti-smoking publicity barely existed. A rise in deaths due to lung cancer can be expected in these countries whereas the advanced economies will continue to see falls in such deaths.

6. ***Exploitation of workers***

   There is little doubt that workers employed by multinationals in developing countries enjoy lower wages, conditions and protection than those employed in advanced economies. Health and safety standards are weaker and long hours are worked. The pay received for sewing a garment may be less than 1% of the retail price it attains in the advanced economy.

7. ***Use of child labour***

   Even when multinationals make clear that they do not want child labour employed they are unable to monitor the activities of their suppliers closely at all times. Investigative television reporting revealed that the sequins on the cheap clothing of one major UK discount chain could have been sewn on by children.

8. ***Unskilled workers in advanced economies face competition***

   For UK workers, having knowledge and skills has never been more important. Unskilled and semi-skilled jobs have been exported to developing countries along with swathes of manufacturing. Wages in unskilled jobs come under pressure from foreign workers who can undercut them.

9. ***Recessions may become global***

   When the world economy is interlinked, the danger of a recession affecting the whole globe at the same time is greater. When Europe and the USA start buying less, then China will produce less and so recession is quickly exported. This would be the theory, but you may care to check whether China's economy shrunk in the aftermath of the 2007-08 financial crisis.

10. ***Environmental damage***

    Weak and corrupt government can leave the door open for environmental damage to forests and agricultural land. For example, mining can be very polluting and modern fishing methods may ruin stocks.

Globalisation advantages and disadvantages

Go online 

Q8: Put the following advantages and disadvantages of globalisation into the correct column in the table below:

- Destruction of traditional agricultural communities;
- Dramatic reductions in costs of production;
- Easier spread of disease;
- Environmental damage;
- Exploitation of workers;
- Extension of democracy;
- Greater knowledge of and respect for other cultures;
- Improved environmental performance;
- Improvements in life expectancy;
- Improvements in literacy rates;
- Improvements in standards of living;
- Improvements in working conditions;
- Increased international cooperation;
- Movement of skilled workers to richest countries;
- Problems associated with the restructuring of economies;
- Recessions may become global;
- The spread of new technology;
- Unskilled workers in advanced economies face competition;
- Use of child labour;
- Widening gap between richest and poorest countries.

Advantages	Disadvantages

4.6 Globalisation: the Chinese experience

It is over a quarter of a century since communist China introduced free market reforms. Chinese Prime Minister, Mr Wen Jiabao, praised the Scottish eighteenth century economist Adam Smith in speeches and meetings with western journalists. He informed the Financial Times that he was carrying Smith's 'The Theory of Moral Sentiments' in his suitcase.

Mr Wen Jiabao was particularly keen on the section that explains that economic development must be shared by all otherwise it is "morally unsound" as well as threatening social stability.

Adam Smith's work

As an advanced higher student, you may be interested in accessing Adam Smith's work 'The Theory of Moral Sentiments'. The full text will be available on the internet, or you could read one of the summaries.

This is not relevant to your current topic of globalisation and is entirely optional.

China's approach to globalisation has been cautious. Initially China protected its huge home market which hardly makes it a typical example of globalisation at work. Since joining the WTO (World Trade Organisation), China has opened itself to more trade. However international trade remains a small proportion of the overall Chinese economy.

China's strategy has been to offer a low-wage manufacturing base to attract foreign investment. The coastal area of China has done far better than the vast inland provinces. China's rapid economic growth has led to overcapacity in many industries. The impact has been felt in other countries with corporate profits falling and the formation of defensive mergers to eliminate competition.

In 2014 economic growth was 7%. Halfway through 2015 the annualised growth in factory output was 6%. Investment in fixed assets (often property) has grown at 11%.

These figures are a slowdown, but nowhere near a recession.

China has responded to market conditions by cutting interest rates and taking steps to boost domestic demand and increase imports. They claim to be moving towards a more market-based economic system by offering shares in giant state-owned conglomerates to private investors.

China's economy Go online

Q9: What would attract multinational companies to China?

....

Q10: Which statistic above suggests that living standards in China are growing rapidly?

India's economy

Q11: Investigate how globalisation has impacted on India.

4.7 Summary

Summary

You should now be able to:

- explain the concept of globalisation;
- analyse the benefits of globalisation and the problems it may bring;
- analyse the reasons (including globalisation) for the rapid economic growth of China;
- research effectively a wide range of economic data.

4.8 End of topic test

End of Topic 4 test Go online

Q12: Claimed benefits of globalisation do ***not*** include:

a) longer life expectancy.
b) increased literacy rates.
c) a reduction in global warming.
d) the spread of modern technology.

....

Q13: As a result of globalisation, you would expect increases in:

a) tariffs.
b) labour mobility.
c) costs of production.
d) all of the above.

....

Q14: Globalisation describes a process that has come about through:

a) the lowering of transport costs due to containerisation.
b) the growth of global brands marketed internationally.
c) improvements in communication technology.
d) all of the above.

....

Q15: Analyse the impact of globalisation on the UK economy. *(20 marks)*

Unit 2 Topic 5

Global economic issues: the European Union

Contents

Prerequisites

This topic assumes no previous knowledge and is intended to be accessible for those studying Economics for the first time. However, if you have already completed Higher Economics you will be familiar with some of the concepts outlined.

Learning objective

By the end of this topic you should be able to:

- analyse the problems facing the eurozone;
- understand the difficulties faced by any nation leaving the eurozone;
- analyse the benefits and disadvantages of joining the eurozone;
- discuss the benefits and disadvantages of further EU enlargement with particular reference to Turkey;
- explain the aims of reforms to the Common Agricultural Policy;
- research effectively and analyse a wide range of economic data.

5.1 Introduction

This topic, as with other topics in this subject, has been selected in the expectation that it will continue to be a topical issue in Economics for some years ahead. It provides useful background on the EU which is expected to continue to throw up opportunities for dissertation topics in the future. For example, at the time of writing the possible exit of Greece from the **euro** would be a topical issue.

Be aware of the need to use up-to-date source material to supplement the information here. You will also need to monitor with your teacher whether this topic does, as hoped, remain relevant for some years.

The original six EU countries have gradually grown to 28 members. as shown in the table below.

Year	Nations Joining	Total Membership
1957	Belgium, France, Italy, Luxembourg, Netherlands, West Germany	6
1973	Denmark, Eire, United Kingdom	9
1981	Greece	10
1986	Portugal, Spain	12
1995	Austria, Finland, Sweden	15
2004	Cyprus, Czech Republic, Estonia, Hungary, Latvia, Lithuania, Malta, Poland, Slovakia, Slovenia	25
2007	Bulgaria, Rumania	27
2013	Croatia	28

EU enlargement

Expansion of the EU Go online 

Q1: Which 11 EU countries adopted the euro in 1999? Find this information using a reliable source on the internet.

....

Q2: Which eight countries had joined these 11 countries in the eurozone by early 2015?

5.2 Pressures on the eurozone

Since their economies converged and many of the nations of Europe adopted the single currency, economic divergence in the **eurozone** has increased again. This has brought pressures on the euro single currency that have been accentuated by recession in 2009. This issue for the eurozone is likely to remain topical for some years.

The pressures facing the eurozone are:

1. The single currency requires a single interest rate throughout the eurozone. For Spain, Greece and Ireland this interest rate was too low to quell inflationary, overheating economies. Germany, on the other hand, could have a lower interest rate. German unit labour costs rose only 5% over the euro's first decade, but Greek unit labour costs went up by 35%. In Spain and Italy, unit labour costs rose by 25%. What this clearly indicates is economies that are diverging. Under the old multi-currency system, the German mark would revalue and the Greek drachma would devalue; but this is no longer possible. Greek exports stay less competitive.

2. The fiscal position of the various governments has also been diverging. The weaker countries may need the support of the stronger countries. Greece has to pay far more than Germany to borrow money. Lending to the Greek government is considered riskier, so the interest rate is higher to reflect this. (It is worth noting that before the euro it was not unusual for the interest rate differential to be high - as much as 6% higher for the 1990s Italian economy.)

European Central Bank (ECB) Go online 

Research the euro by visiting the European Central Bank (ECB) website (http://bit.ly/1bgDXvk) and find the link for 'The Euro'.

5.2.1 The immediate outlook for the euro

Will countries quit the euro? Or will they find policies that enable them to re-establish **convergence**? Or will they just suffer economically for several years without effective policies to lift their economies, but determined to stay inside the euro. These are the three possible outcomes.

At the time of writing Greece appears to have chosen the third option, but it is possible that they may yet quit the euro. The IMF are trying to press them into economic policies that might help them re-establish convergence.

Leaving the euro seems unlikely. Politically, the negative fallout of withdrawing from the euro would seem likely to hit governments hard at the polls. It would seem like an admission of failure, even of second-class status, and would be hard to sell to voters, especially as it would seem to come as a last resort. Economics often takes a back seat to politics.

5.2.2 Leaving the euro or re-establishing convergence

Precedents in leaving a single currency

There are precedents in leaving a single currency. The Czech Republic split from Slovakia and their single currency separated. There have been similar experiences in the break-up of the old Yugoslavia. There are perhaps even parallels with the Irish Republic which maintained parity for the punt with sterling for many years (until 1979).

So, the break-up of common currencies is not new. It can happen and shouldn't be dismissed. Particularly, as a deep recession can lead to seismic political changes, and it is feasible that an election in one country could be won by an outsider or newcomer proposing to leave the euro.

Costs of leaving the euro

However, leaving the euro presents some practical problems in terms of cost:

- It is likely that only a nation in considerable economic difficulties would want to leave the euro. This could cause its new currency to decline in value from the moment of issue. The exchange rate at creation would have to be defendable, or the speculators would move in to make a killing. Supporting the new currency (devalued at birth) would be expensive. A life jacket from the IMF or the World Bank would be required, and they would only give help if the country reformed its economy (e.g. labour markets, privatisation) and reduced its fiscal deficit. If the country could do that, it wouldn't have to leave the euro in the first place;
- Borrowing money against this unstable economic backdrop would be expensive. The government would have to pay high interest rates;
- Vending machines may require modification, although it is possible to have new currency of the same size and weight as the euro. Computers would need reprogramming - the keyboards will need to produce a new currency symbol;
- A run on the banks of those leaving the euro is a big risk. The currency value would be redenominated on the changeover day, and the international value of the new denomination may plummet. Investors would seek a safe haven for their money in an established and stable currency. The already weak government fiscal position that would be part of the reason for leaving the euro would not help the government to bail out the banks.

Leaving the euro smoothly would take a lot of planning and some good fortune.

Re-establishing convergence

A far more likely outcome is that nations will remain in the euro but put their economies through a painful adjustment process. For an example of this, look at the 2009 Irish budget and the wholesale fiscal adjustments made in it. The danger here is that aggregate demand will fall further, worsening the recession. Then, the fiscal position may further deteriorate with unemployment and social benefits rising against a background of falling tax receipts.

If re-establishing convergence with the stronger euro economies is difficult, the third outcome is long-term stagnation for the weaker members. A period of low economic growth will follow unless the stronger economies boost their consumption with a large fiscal stimulus.

Other more extreme possibilities include some governments defaulting on debt, and choosing either to stay with or leave the euro in the aftermath.

Single currency options Go online 

Q3: Research information on the options available for nations wishing to leave the eurozone. A starting point may be to search online for "should Greece leave the Euro?"

....

Q4: Search the web to find an article that explains how Czechoslovakia divided its currency into two separate currencies when it split into the Czech Republic and Slovakia.

5.3 The advantages and disadvantages of euro membership

Benefits of euro membership include:

1. ***Transaction costs*** - There will be no costs involved in changing currencies. Firms and tourists will benefit from this. Attempts to quantify this benefit suggest a once and for all gain of about 1% of GDP.
2. **Price transparency** - It will be easier to compare prices throughout the eurozone because they would all be in euros. Firms and consumers would find cheaper raw materials and goods. With a single currency consumers would notice these price differentials and firms would come under pressure to reduce them.
3. ***Reducing exchange rate uncertainty*** - Firms trading with, but not in, the eurozone have enough uncertainty to handle with normal business risk and economic cycles. At present, over and above these risks, there is the chance of the euro exchange rate moving against them and ruining profits all on its own. Joining the euro single currency reduces the risk from volatile exchange rates and should lead to greater trade and economic growth.
4. ***Reducing the risk of inflation*** - The theory was that German discipline (paranoia?) about inflation would ensure that the European Central Bank would set a strong line with interest rates to confine inflation.
5. ***Inward investment*** - If the plan is to export to the eurozone, then this should be more attractive without transaction costs and with no exchange rate volatility.
6. ***Impact on the financial sector*** - Trading in eurozone shares would be made easier. Insurance and banking would have a similar opportunity to develop in foreign markets.

The disadvantages include:

1. ***Loss of independent control of monetary policy*** - The European Central Bank and the interest rate it sets could be out of line with a particular nation's economic needs.
2. ***Impact on the housing market*** - In the case of UK entry, the significance of interest rate changes for the UK economy is greater because of the UK's focus on house purchase rather than rental. This adds weight to the argument for the UK to retain control of interest rates by not joining the eurozone.
3. ***Changeover costs*** - The initial costs of changing currency are large - vending and slot machine changes are one example.
4. ***Loss of devaluation option*** - Devaluation is removed from a nation's economic policy options, so they would no longer be able to stimulate their economy by devaluing the currency and increasing exports. If they can't remain convergent with stronger economies (if for example wage costs rise) it will need to deflationary fiscal policies to compensate. The euro is essentially a fixed exchange rate arrangement, and in time may be subject to the same pressures from diverging economies that fixed rates have always been subject to. With the added pressure of recession, Spain, Portugal and Greece would all have benefitted from a lower exchange rate relative to other countries, but no such option existed for them.
5. ***Loss of independent fiscal policy*** - The EU's growth and stability pact would limit government borrowing to 3% of GDP. Increased regional aid within Europe will be needed

to offset economic inequalities that can no longer be addressed through national currency realignments. Richer nations will be net contributors to this funding. If some eurozone members increase their borrowings and national debt, this will lead to the single interest rate rising throughout the zone.

6. ***Unexpected events*** - Over time, a number of unexpected events can be expected. These events will be of different significance for each eurozone economy. They will make these economies diverge. For example, the "credit crunch" had a disproportionate effect on countries such as the UK and Ireland where the banking and financial sectors are a larger part of the total economy. If oil prices soared then net importers of oil such as France and Germany would be far more affected than the UK with its North Sea production. Policy responses for these "shocks" could usefully involve interest rates, but within the one size fits all eurozone interest rates, this option is not available.

Advantages and disadvantages of joining the eurozone Go online 

Q5: Decide whether the following statements are advantages or disadvantages of joining the eurozone:

- Devaluation of national currency no longer possible;
- Easier for consumers to compare prices in different countries;
- Exchange rate certainty for firms within eurozone;
- Fiscal policy subject to strict rules that limit ability to borrow in recession;
- Multinational investment more likely;
- No commission on changing currency;
- One interest rate set for all of eurozone;
- Unexpected events may lead to eurozone economies diverging.

Advantages	Disadvantages

5.4 EU enlargement

EU **enlargement** is the process of widening the EU through the admission of new members. The EU project started in 1957 with six member states and now it has enlarged six times and by 2015 it had 28 member nations.

Around the edges of the current map, the Balkan states formed on the break-up Yugoslavia will shortly be looking for entry (e.g. Serbia). Turkey has long been interested, but is perhaps not as close to membership now as a few years ago. North African countries just across the Mediterranean have historic links to many European countries and are also possible members.

Switzerland retains an independent outlook and has historically sought to remain neutral, with secretive Swiss banks perhaps preferring not to have European Union laws applied to them. Norway voted against entry when its Scandinavian neighbours joined. It has a small population similar to Scotland and its immense oil reserves make it very prosperous outside the EU. Also, its important fishing industry does not have to abide by EU policies.

5.4.1 Recent EU enlargement

When Romania and Bulgaria joined the EU in 2007, the European Commission said that they brought the following advantages:

- rapidly growing economies - about 6% a year;
- a highly motivated workforce;
- a potential link between the EU and Balkan and Black Sea areas.

Romania and Bulgaria have 6% of the EU population and less than 1% of the EU GDP. They are the poorest members of the EU with GDP per head running at a third of the EU average. Entry was allowed despite concerns over corruption and organised crime, the assumption being that allowing them in would assist reform in these areas.

Future candidates for membership include:

- Albania;
- Bosnia and Herzegovina;
- Kosovo;
- Macedonia;
- Montenegro;
- Serbia;
- Turkey.

EU treaties allow any European country to apply if it meets conditions, such as:

- a market economy;
- the rule of law;
- respect for human rights;
- democracy.

5.4.2 The case for and against EU enlargement

Following entry, new members receive more from the EU than they pay into the budget. Bulgaria and Romania received about 1.5bn euros in pre-entry assistance.

However, many of the older EU members (e.g. Spain, Greece, Portugal and Ireland) also end up with net gains from membership. In fact, Spain received more in 2005 than the 10 new member states combined.

There are greater gains for all from membership of the **single market** that are far more significant than making a net gain from the EU budget and these do not enter the calculations.

Benefits of EU enlargement

The process of enlargement has several benefits for the UK:

- provides consumers with a greater choice of products, as new members begin to export to the UK;
- increases competition which drives down prices, leads to innovative behaviour by firms and can improve the quality of products;
- allows labour shortages to be met with foreign workers. This addition to supply in the labour market will help to keep down wage inflation, which is good news for companies and a benefit for the overall economy;
- provides new markets (no trade barriers) for our exports and exporters should gain more from economies of scale as they supply a free trade single market of nearly 500 million consumers;
- provides opportunities for UK-based firms to improve profitability by moving to the lower wage economies of the new members.

Problems with EU enlargement

The process of enlargement also creates problems for the UK:

- UK workers will face more competition in the labour market and their wages are less likely to rise. (However, unemployment may not rise, because much of the money earned by foreign workers will be spent in the UK and thus they create jobs as well as take jobs.)
- subsidies for the economic development of the new members may be expensive for richer countries such as the UK. The UK will be a net contributor to the EU budget through the CAP and regional aid.
- firms may move manufacturing to the new member countries to take advantage of lower costs (e.g. wages) and this will lead to some job losses in the UK.

EU enlargement Go online 

Put the following words into place in the paragraph below:

- choice;
- competition;
- foreign workers;
- job losses;
- manufacturing;
- prices;

- profitability;
- quality;
- subsidies;
- wages.

Q6: For the UK the process of enlargement has several benefits. Consumers will have a greater .... of products. This increases .... which drives down .... , leads to innovative behaviour by firms, and can improve the .... of products. Enlargement allows labour shortages to be met with .... and keeps down wage inflation. It provides opportunities for UK based firms to improve .... by moving to the lower wage economies of the new members.

Enlargement can create problems. UK workers will face more competition in the labour market and their .... are less likely to rise. Regional aid and CAP .... for the economic development of the new members may be expensive. Firms may move .... and some service jobs to the new member countries to take advantage of lower wages and this will lead to some .... in the UK.

5.4.3 Turkey

Of all the potential entrants, Turkey provides the most interesting case. The remaining non-EU European nations have fairly small populations and while the political operation and decision-making of an increasingly numerous EU state count may be difficult, at least from an economic viewpoint the absorption of these countries should follow established models.

The Helsinki European Council of December 1999 granted Turkey candidate status. Accession negotiations started in October 2005 after reforms that included:

- the abolition of the death penalty;
- protections against torture;
- greater freedom of expression and increased respect for minorities.

Turkey is special, and worthy of study as a case on its own, as:

1. it links Europe to Asia;
2. its democracy has looked unstable at times and EU membership would entrench democracy in Turkey. This would improve stability, security and prosperity in that region;
3. it is a populous nation that, with a market economy and globalisation, has the potential to be a significant economic power;
4. it provides links to energy sources to the East;
5. it greatly expands the single market and embraces globalisation for existing EU members. Politically, the EU acting as one would be an even more powerful block.

There are stumbling blocks. For example, further progress is required on:

- women's rights;
- anti-corruption measures;
- judicial reform;
- agricultural reform;
- freedom of expression and the rights of minority religious groups.

Turkey also does not recognise Cyprus and this means it cannot open its ports and airports to all EU member states.

Turkey - EU membership Go online 

Q7: Summarise the benefits that the membership of Turkey may bring to the EU. *(6 marks)*

....

Q8: Summarise the outstanding issues that have to be dealt with before the EU will give final consideration to Turkey's application. *(6 marks)*

Turkey's current economic performance Go online 

Q9: Investigate the current economic performance of Turkey by going to the CIA World Factbook (http://1.usa.gov/1FY6ErF) .

Make notes on the variations between the economic and social data on Turkey compared to a major EU country such as Germany.

5.5 Reform of the Common Agricultural Policy (CAP)

The **Common Agricultural Policy (CAP)** is the biggest item of EU expenditure, costing the UK several billion a year in subsidy and increasing food costs. It uses up a large proportion of the EU budget. France enjoys the largest share of CAP funds. Ireland and Greece also receive a large share, relative to their economic size.

The CAP hits the world's poorest countries by subsidising their high-cost competitors in the EU. It does not adequately protect the natural environment. Much of the money goes to agribusiness and not to the poorest farmers.

Subsidised products include olives, fruit, vegetables, sugar and wine. Costs running into billions of euros are paid to olive farmers and to sugar producers. In one year the biggest gainer from the CAP in the UK was the sugar company Tate and Lyle with a donation from the EU of €186 million. The Queen has received approximately €500,000 per year!

The subsidies distort world markets and harm farmers in developing countries by guaranteeing good prices for farmers in the EU. For further protection, tariffs are added to the price of imports.

One notorious example of an EU subsidy was in the sugar market. The world price for sugar was £144 per tonne, but the EU had a minimum guaranteed price of £432 - almost three times as much.

Recent changes build on a major CAP reform process started in 2003. This broke the link between farm production and subsidies. The current objective is to move funding into rural development and conservation measures and to leave agriculture more responsive to market forces.

Reform of the EU intends to encourage farmers to move away from dependency on subsidies and promote sustainable and diverse rural communities.

Common Agricultural Policy (CAP) 

Research the latest information on reform of the CAP. The official EU website (http://europa.eu/index_en.htm) is a useful starting point.

5.6 Summary

Summary

You should now be able to:

- analyse the problems facing the eurozone;
- understand the difficulties faced by any nation leaving the eurozone;
- analyse the benefits and disadvantages of joining the eurozone;
- discuss the benefits and disadvantages of further EU enlargement with particular reference to Turkey;
- explain the aims of reforms to the Common Agricultural Policy;
- research effectively and analyse a wide range of economic data.

5.7 End of topic test

End of topic 5 test Go online

Q10: Which country joined the EU in 2013?

a) Switzerland
b) Russia
c) Croatia
d) Norway

....

Q11: How many nations are currently (2015) in the EU?

a) 15
b) 21
c) 25
d) 28

....

Q12: Which of the following nations was a founding member of the EU?

a) Italy
b) United Kingdom
c) Spain
d) Denmark

....

Q13: Which two countries joined the EU in 2007?

a) Slovenia and Slovakia
b) Latvia and Lithuania
c) Romania and Bulgaria
d) Croatia and Serbia

....

Q14: The initials CAP stand for:

a) Current Agricultural Policy
b) Common Agricultural Policy
c) Current Accession Procedure
d) Common Accession Procedure

....

Q15: EU enlargement refers to the process of:

a) creating of a greater number of common standards throughout the EU.
b) economic growth creating greater European gross domestic product.
c) establishing wider powers for the European Parliament.
d) the widening of the EU by allowing in new member nations.

....

Q16: Which of the following (as of 2015) is a eurozone member state?

a) United Kingdom
b) Portugal
c) Sweden
d) Denmark

....

Q17: Two problems with allowing Turkey to join the EU is that: *(choose the two options that apply)*

a) part of Turkey is in Asia.
b) the death penalty still exists in Turkey.
c) further progress is required on women's rights.
d) it must become a democracy first.

....

Q18: One advantage for the UK in joining the eurozone is the ability to:

a) devalue the currency so as to compete better in the eurozone.
b) set interest rates to suit the needs of our economy.
c) easily compare UK prices with those of other eurozone nations.
d) budget for a large fiscal deficit if the economy requires it.

Unit 2 Topic 6

Economic growth in developing and emerging economies

Contents

Learning objective

By the end of this topic you should be able to:

- explain reasons for varying rates of economic growth in developing economies;
- explain reasons for varying rates of economic growth in emerging economies;
- research effectively and analyse a wide range of economic data.

6.1 Emerging economies

There is no established convention on the definition of the terms **developing economy** and **emerging economy**. Also, many similar terms co-exist, e.g. least developed economies, tiger economies, BRIC economies.

One recent addition to the terms used to describe emerging economies is 'EAGLES' which is an acronym for Emerging and Growth Leading Economies. This current EAGLE membership, in the table below, provides a useful list for our term emerging economies.

Bangladesh	Nigeria
Brazil	Pakistan
China	Philippines
India	Russia
Indonesia	Saudi Arabia
Iraq	Thailand
Mexico	Turkey

EAGLE membership (as of 2014)

For the purposes of this course there are three divisions broadly judged by their GDP per capita, viz:

- advanced economies (e.g. USA);
- emerging economies (e.g. Brazil);
- developing economies (e.g. Malawi).

Many countries are transitioning up the divisions, and therefore it is best to select clear-cut examples as above and to avoid the grey areas of transition in between.

An emerging economy is a nation with some characteristics of an advanced economy but is not yet an advanced economy. These nations have business and economic activity in the process of rapid growth and industrialization. They are clearly more prosperous than developing economies as can be judged by statistics for GDP per capita, literacy rates and life expectancy rates.

World factbook - emerging economies Go online 

Q1: Find the GDP per capita of Brazil and India using the World Factbook section of the CIA website (http://1.usa.gov/1KyForg).

Then find two other 'EAGLE' nations with broadly similar GDP per capita figures.

6.2 Developing economies

According to the International Monetary Fund's World Economic Outlook Report (April 2015) there are 152 countries considered to be developing economies (http://bit.ly/1JwEGIL).

Immediately, we have a definition problem. The IMF (International Monetary Fund), the World Bank and the United Nations are just three of the august institutions that cannot agree on a definition of the terms in this area. Hence the list of countries is of limited use.

World factbook - developing economies Go online 

Q2: Find the GDP per capita of Malawi and Chad using the World Factbook section of the CIA website (http://1.usa.gov/1KyForg).

Then find two other nations from the list of developing economies with broadly similar GDP per capita figures.

6.3 Factors that delay economic growth

When it comes to the problems facing less developed countries, one approach is to take the four factors of production in turn and recite quality and quantity issues they face.

The following may give you an initial understanding of the roots of their problems:

- **Natural resources** (Land) will not be fertile. Either the climate or the soil type will prevent it from producing plenty. If it is fertile, then it may be prone to seasonal flooding or drought. Crop yields will either be low or not reliable. Agriculture will dominate many of these economies with perhaps 80% of the workforce engaged in farming.

  Mineral deposits will be limited or difficult to access. Those mines that do exist will be owned by multinationals and the workers may be poorly paid with the profits going to shareholders in developed countries. Political instability and corruption may prevent the returns from valuable mineral deposits trickling down to the general population.

- **Human resources** (Labour) will not be skilled. The education system will be poor and literacy rates low. As a result, labour productivity will be low and foreign investment will not be attracted other than to exploit valuable mineral deposits. Workers may be weakened by malnutrition or disease.

  Life expectancy will be low. There may be a burgeoning young population of dependents but quite a small population of working age. The number of able workers of working age will be restricted by health issues. In many parts, HIV and Aids are significantly affecting many families.

- **Man-made resources** (Capital) will be of poor quality. Operating at near subsistence level there will be no surplus put aside to assist with future production. Machinery will tend to be cheap and basic when it does exist. The lack of social capital and infrastructure such as roads and harbours will make the country unattractive to foreign investors.

  A lack of savings will lead to a lack of funds being recycled into investment. The banking system will be poor. Foreign investment is badly needed to kick-start economic development.

- **Entrepreneurs** (Enterprise) will exist on a small scale in local markets. Any excess farm output will find its way to a market stall. The growth of enterprise is dependent on the availability of capital to invest, and partly on the education levels of the entrepreneurs.

  The number of entrepreneurs and the size of companies will be restricted by the small incomes of consumers, and the inadequacies of the banking system.

These problems with the four factors of production lead to long term problems with economic development.

Factors that delay economic growth Go online 

Q3: Match the following quality and quantity issues to each factor of production in the table below:

- bureaucratic "red tape";
- inadequate roads;
- low rainfall;
- poor health;
- limited skills;
- little savings;
- few business skills;
- few natural resources.

Land	Labour	Capital	Enterprise

6.4 Economic growth and stage of economic development

A brief look at the historic statistics in the table below reveals a pattern. Both emerging and developing economies are growing more rapidly than advanced economies (percentages rounded to nearest half per cent).

Type of economy	2007	2008	2009	2010
Emerging and developing	9%	6%	2.5%	7.5%
Advanced	2.5%	0%	-3.5%	3%
Total world growth	5%	3%	-0.5%	5%

Economic growth and type of economy

Note that the growth rates of emerging and developing countries should not be considered in isolation from population growth. GDP per capita tends to rise more slowly than GDP.

Economic growth of developing and emerging economies Go online 

Q4: Obtain the most up-to-date figures available on the internet for the economic growth of developing and emerging economies.

The important factors that influence the rate of economic growth in developing countries are:

- improvements in education, especially primary education and the accompanying increase in literacy and numeracy;
- improvements in sanitation and health care, which lead to lower infant mortality, increased life expectancy and fitter, more productive workers;
- political stability - improvements in the legal system and an absence of civil war or international conflict;
- diversification away from reliance on a single primary product.

Emerging economies have these pre-conditions for growth in place and continue to improve education and health services. Emerging economies with the highest growth rates will have:

- high levels of private investment in business - much of it from foreign multinationals;
- high levels of investment by government in major infrastructure projects such as improvements to transport links;
- an economy rapidly diversifying into manufacturing;
- moves towards free trade and internationally open markets;
- the encouragement of entrepreneurship and a preference for free market solutions over state intervention;
- relaxed labour laws (workers are poorly protected from exploitation) and very competitive hourly wage rates.

Economic growth of developing and emerging economies Go online 

Q5: What are the three most important pre-conditions for the initial economic growth of developing countries?

....

Q6: Suggest three further factors that contribute to the economic growth of emerging economies.

6.5 Research example - the effect of falling commodity prices on Zambia

Zambia was the world's third largest copper producer in the 1960s. On gaining independence from the UK in 1964, it seemed destined to be one of Africa's most prosperous countries. What happened?

Map showing location of Zambia within Africa

In 1975 the world copper price slumped. Despite the undermining effect this had on the Zambian economy, it remained the country's biggest export earner. Zambia was unable to diversify sufficiently, and although agriculture and tourism also contribute to the economy, the price of copper has remained key to the country's economic development.

From the 1990s, two favourable events have assisted the Zambian copper industry. Firstly, the industry has been privatised, thus releasing the powerful profit motive and opening the door to foreign investment. Secondly, the growth of the worldwide sales of electronics led to a derived increased demand for copper.

The fundamental problem for Zambia and nations in a similar position is the over-dependence on one primary product. Zambia's economy needs to diversify. Until it has diversified, the prosperity of Zambia is closely linked to the volatile world copper price.

The price of copper has not been the only problem facing Zambia in this period. You should be able to research the other issues that faced Zambia, many of which were typical of a less developed country.

Zambia's problems Go online 

Q7: What problems have faced Zambia since independence (1964)?

A good starting point may be the Country Profiles (http://bbc.in/1Lw8tzl) section on the BBC website.

Real GDP growth in Zambia is expected to increase to over 6% in 2015. This resumes previous growth rates following 5.7% in 2013, due to reduced copper production. The country benefits from political stability, and although 60% still live in poverty, the standards of living are improving in cities and along major transport routes. A major aim of government is the diversification of the economy to reduce the dependence on copper.

Highly Indebted Poor Country (HIPC) Initiative Go online 

Q8: Use the internet to find out about the Highly Indebted Poor Country (HIPC) Initiative. How does the HIPC Initiative help these countries?

The price of copper Go online 

Q9: Find out as much as you can about the price of copper over the last few years. Comment on the variations you find.

Another developing economy Go online 

Q10: Find out about another one of the world's developing economies. What are the country's particular economics problems? To what extent does it resemble the Zambian experience?

Your starting point may be the information available through the BBC website's Country Profiles (http://bbc.in/1Lw8tzl) or through the CIA's World Factbook (http://1.usa.gov/1FY6ErF) section.

6.6 Research example - the effect of rising energy prices on developing countries

Surprisingly, some of the world's poorest countries are oil producers. Nigeria has been a well-known oil producer for years. Less well-known are the oil reserves of Angola, Chad, Sudan and Equatorial Guinea.

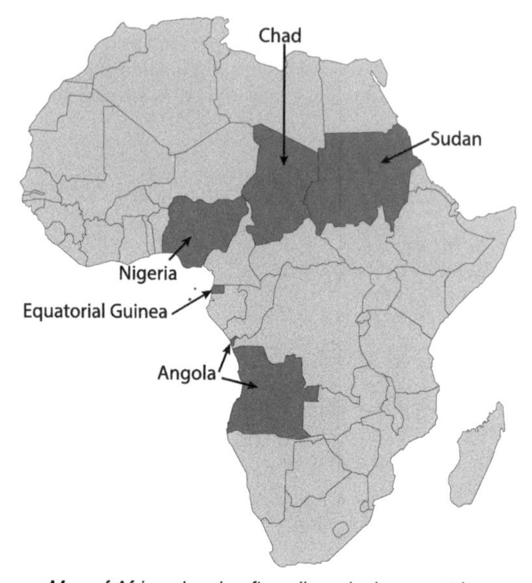

Map of Africa showing five oil producing countries

The rise in energy prices should have helped these countries, but did they make good use of the extra revenues?

Equatorial Guinea is now the third largest oil exporter in sub-Saharan Africa. Despite this, most of its small population live in poverty. The same president has been in office since 1979, and the ruling elite are prosperous. According to the International Monetary Fund, Angola had no records for about $4 billion of oil revenues for the period 1997 and 2002.

Even when corruption is not the issue, these countries can lack expertise in allocating the revenues to sensible investments in infrastructure. Rising oil prices have also been blamed for increasing power struggles within these countries.

For the greater number of poor countries the problems of rising energy prices represent an intolerable additional burden, rather than the windfall they are to Angola and the oil exporters.

By 2007, oil prices had tripled in four years. In the Asian and Pacific region, this put spending on imports up by nearly $400 billion. One study of the impact on the poor in these areas states that spending on energy went up by three quarters between 2002 and 2005. The poor are faced with cutting back on other essentials in order to pay for basics such as lighting and cooking oil.

Nations with the greatest dependence on imported oil include Cambodia and Sri Lanka. Less dependent but still vulnerable are Malaysia and Thailand because of their rapidly growing demand for oil. China and India face less of a problem because of their greater use of coal, and their stronger economies can face the challenge of higher oil prices.

The effect of rising oil prices on developing countries Go online 

Q11: Explain the effect of rising oil prices on developing countries.

6.7 Summary

Summary

You should now be able to:

- explain reasons for varying rates of economic growth in developing economies;
- explain reasons for varying rates of economic growth in emerging economies;
- research effectively and analyse a wide range of economic data.

6.8 End of topic test

End of Topic 6 test Go online 

Q12: Which of the following countries have emerging economies? Choose ***five*** countries.

Brazil	Chad	China	India	Ireland
Italy	Malawi	Mali	Nigeria	Russia

Choose the best option to complete the following sentences regarding developing countries.

Q13: Developing countries make progress if they are able to improve the ....

a) birthrate
b) levels of literacy and numeracy
c) natural resources

....

Q14: More productive workers are possible if .... levels are improved.

a) welfare benefit
b) pension
c) sanitation

....

Q15: The economy will also need to diversify away from a dependence on a single .... product.

a) primary
b) secondary
c) tertiary

....

Q16: Describe the characteristics of emerging economies. *(6 marks)*

Unit 2 Topic 7

National and global economic issues test

National and global economic issues test

Go online 

Q1: The structural deficit exists because of:

a) increased benefit spending during recession.
b) reduced income tax receipts during recession.
c) long-term investment in infrastructure by government.
d) the privatisation of public sector assets.

....

Q2: The demand for oil depends on:

a) the weather in oil-producing regions.
b) political stability in oil-producing nations.
c) economic growth around the world.
d) changes in capital allowances that reduce taxes on oil.

....

Q3: Lower oil prices could benefit the UK economy by:

i. reducing inflationary pressure.
ii. increasing consumption in other areas of the economy.
iii. improving productivity in the North Sea.

a) i) and ii) only
b) i) and iii) only
c) ii) and iii) only
d) all of the above

....

Q4: As a result of globalisation, you would expect increases in:

a) tariffs.
b) labour mobility.
c) costs of production.
d) all of the above.

....

Q5: Globalisation describes a process that has come about through:

a) the lowering of transport costs due to containerisation.
b) the growth of global brands marketed internationally.
c) improvements in communication technology.
d) all of the above.

....

Q6: Greece may find it difficult to be in a common currency with Germany because:

a) the cost of transporting their exports to Germany is high.
b) they do not share a central bank.
c) inflation in Germany tends to be higher.
d) they cannot match German levels of productivity.

....

Q7: By ***not*** being in the Eurozone, the UK is able to:

a) impose tariffs on imports from the Eurozone.
b) avoid currency conversion costs.
c) set its own interest rates independently.
d) limit the free movement of labour from the Eurozone.

....

Q8: Economic growth in developing economies can be held back by:

I. poor health and sanitation.
II. low levels of spending on education.
III. high government spending on infrastructure projects.

a) I) and II) only
b) I) and III) only
c) II) and III) only
d) I), II) and III)

....

Q9: Economic growth in emerging economies is encouraged by:

I. increasing levels of foreign investment.
II. high spending on education.
III. political stability.

a) I) and II) only
b) I) and III) only
c) II) and III) only
d) I), II) and III)

....

Q10: Which of the following groups lists a developing economy, an emerging economy, and an advanced economy in that order?

a) Russia, Japan, Germany
b) Malawi, Brazil, Canada
c) India, Zambia, France
d) China, Mali, Italy

....

Q11: Explain how "austerity" policies that reduce government spending could potentially delay the achievement of a balanced budget. *(7 marks)*

. . . .

Q12: Explain the possible benefits for the UK economy of a balanced budget. *(6 marks)*

Researching an economic issue

Unit 3 Topic 1

How to organise your project

Contents

Prerequisites

This topic assumes no previous knowledge and is intended to be accessible for those studying Economics for the first time. However, if you have already completed Higher Economics you will be familiar with some of the concepts outlined.

Learning objective

By the end of this topic you should be able to:

- understand the importance for your project of preparation and planning, and the need for good time management;
- select a suitable topic that is feasible to research and within your capabilities;
- research your chosen topic and analyse your research;
- plan and record a programme of economic research;
- present your project findings in an acceptable structure that relates to the marking scheme;
- synthesise your research into coherent conclusions and present these appropriately.

1.1 Organisation and planning

This project produces an end document which will be an extended piece of writing that is divided into sections. You might make up your own structure, but in Advanced Higher Economics there is guidance supplied on how the marks are allocated which it would be wise to act upon.

Your project will amass the evidence from a wide range of sources that will help you to draw informed economic conclusions to a question that relates to a topical economic issue.

The section you are undertaking when you write your project is called 'researching an economic issue'. It is one of three sections in the Advanced Higher Economics course. The SQA guidance says that "the general aim of this unit is to allow learners to plan their research of a current economic issue in order to develop their economic research skills."

Your project amounts to one third of your final mark.

The good candidate will seek out their teacher for guidance, opinions and criticism. The project allows the well-organised candidate to allocate the time and effort necessary to producing a good quality piece of work. There will be sufficient time for the first draft to be checked over carefully and improved. The final document will be well-presented and standardised in style and layout. Facts will be rigorously checked for accuracy. Conclusions will be subtle and matched up with the initial aims of the project.

The rushed candidate will leave more to chance and may have no clear timetable or make minimal effort to keep to the timetable they have. As the deadline nears they will panic and their research, instead of being wide-ranging, will be aimed at finding one or two items that are ripe for plagiarising. Even if they are sufficiently talented writers, the final outcome is likely to be unsatisfying from an educational point of view and the mark will be less than they might have expected. They will have gained little from the process and they may take away the notion that they can handle future deadlines in this way.

Consider the following:

- Passing the Advanced Higher Economics course with 50% following a project that gains 30/40 requires an examination mark of 30/80 (or 37.5%).
- However, passing the course with 50% following a project that gains 15/40 requires an examination mark of 45/80 (or 56%).
- So, the high-scoring project will put you into the final exam with over a grade advantage over the weaker project. Your university entrance may depend on it - so start early and keep to your dissertation timetable.

Before going any further refer to the SQA documentation on this project at http://www.sqa.org.uk/files_ccc/AHCourseSpecEconomics.pdf.

1.2 Stages in writing up your project

The diagram below gives a simple outline of the stages you will go through in writing your project.

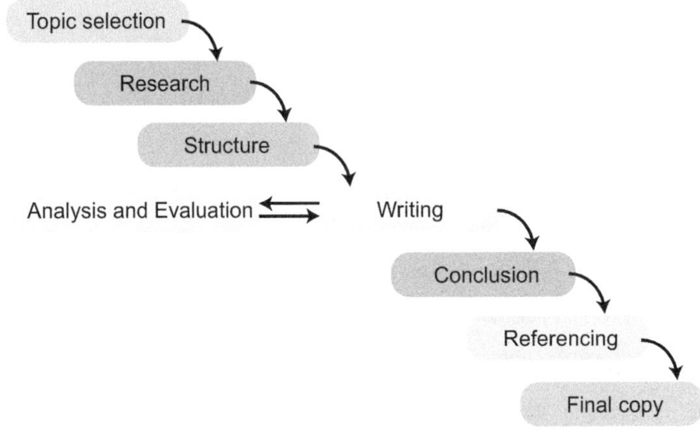

Diagram showing the stages in writing up a project

Placing the elements of the process in a sequential order does over-simplify the procedure a bit. In Economics, you may be dealing with a topic that is developing as you write. Be prepared to adjust and insert new research information as you write. Stay flexible - your final copy will be amended and improved as a result of the evaluation of your draft copy and the incorporation of information acquired late in the day.

Project plan Go online 

Q1: Devise a basic project plan using the broad stages in the diagram above and placing a timescale against them.

1.3 Project remit

You should receive from your teacher:

- clear guidance on the upper and lower word limits;
- advice on the suitability of topics you are considering;
- some pointers on the location of suitable material for starting your research;
- the deadline date for completion (and the teacher may suggest some interim dates for the completion of different stages of the work such as the completion of a first draft).

If you want a considered opinion on your work, you will have to give your teacher sufficient time to look over your draft. This will mean you will have to meet the agreed interim deadlines. Your teacher will have many other students competing for his or her time; don't assume your teacher will give you a privileged status as an Advanced Higher candidate.

Key points for your remit:

- select an economic issue that is topical within the last 18 months;
- word count is between 3500 to 4000 words (excluding bibliography, footnotes and appendices);
- a maximum of three appendices can be included;
- confirm the due date and submit your report by this date;
- have a question as your title, rather than a statement;
- provide references for quotes and tables and graphs;
- a **bibliography** should indicate all sources of information used;
- provide a word count with the report (and a penalty is applied if it exceeds 4,400).

SQA allocate 40 marks for the project, out of a total of 120 marks for the Advanced Higher Economics course. The allocation of marks (in brackets) is broken down as follows:

1. Introduction (3);
2. Analysis and evaluation (18);
3. Conclusions (6);
4. Research (4);
5. Structure and coherence (6);
6. Presentation and referencing (3).

Further details can be accessed at the SQA website (http://www.sqa.org.uk/files_ccc/AHCourseSpecEconomics.pdf).

1.4 Selecting a topic

You should choose a topic that interests you and is within your capabilities. Always check on the ease with which you can research your topic.

The selected issue must be a current issue defined as active within the last two years.

What you don't want to produce is a mere descriptive work. This kind of report may be well-informed, represent a summary of the reading and months of studious activity, and it may show that you have a clear understanding of the topic. However it will probably lack incisiveness, individuality and personal insight. It will be an erudite study or review of the work of others, and more than a little dull.

In Advanced Higher Economics you should pick a topic that is an argument. This will be a question that lacks a definitive answer but offers several viewpoints to criticise and consider, not least your own one which you will form as your research, analysis and evaluation continues.

Your conclusions will, according to the SQA (http://bit.ly/1Kbm7XD) , "demonstrate valid judgements have been reached that are related to the issue/aim(s), and are based on the analysis and evaluation of the evidence. The reasoning behind the conclusions is fully explained." The weighting attached by you to the various conclusions will represent your informed judgement of the issue.

Selecting a topic

Q2: From the following list of topics, select those that best meet the project requirements:

- The financial crisis of 2007-08 - should the banks have been saved?
- Should the budget deficit be reduced?
- Should the UK join the euro?
- Why did house prices fall in 2008?
- What were the causes of the Great Depression?
- What should be the favoured currency option if Scotland gained independence?
- Is the UK heading for another recession?

There are some hints for this activity which you should look at ***after*** you have selected your suitable topics.

1.5 Key points to consider for your project

In summary, the key points to consider for your project are as follows:

- select a current issue that interests you and phrase it as a question;
- time management is important, so agree deadlines for the completion of sections with your teacher and stick to them;
- research widely and maintain a bibliography. Watch out for developments that occur as you are writing as they may require changes to be made;
- refer closely to the way in which marks are allocated and present your project in a format that seeks to gather in these marks;
- follow the teacher's advice on layout and presentation;
- use economic theory to explain wherever possible;
- draw your conclusions from the evidence and explicitly state how the evidence leads you to your conclusions.

1.6 Summary

Summary

You should now be able to:

- understand the importance for your project of preparation and planning, and the need for good time management;
- select a suitable topic that is feasible to research and within your capabilities;
- research your chosen topic and analyse your research;
- plan and record a programme of economic research;
- present your project findings in an acceptable structure that relates to the marking scheme;
- synthesise your research into coherent conclusions and present these appropriately.

1.7 End of topic test

End of Topic 1 test Go online

Q3: In the marks for the project, what percentage is allocated to presentation and referencing?

a) 7.5%
b) 10%
c) 15%

....

Q4: The maximum word limit for the project is:

a) 3,000
b) 3,500
c) 4,000

....

Q5: What percentage of your final course mark is allocated to your project?

a) 20%
b) 25.5%
c) 33.3%

....

Q6: Your chosen topic must be both:

a) current and economically significant.
b) current and macroeconomic.
c) microeconomic and economically significant.

Unit 3 Topic 2

How to research and write your project

Contents

Prerequisites

This topic assumes no previous knowledge and is intended to be accessible for those studying Economics for the first time. However, if you have already completed Higher Economics you will be familiar with some of the concepts outlined.

Learning objective

By the end of this topic you should be able to:

- develop independent research skills;
- understand the difference between qualitative and quantitative research;
- evaluate if the range of sources used is appropriate for the needs of the research;
- keep an accurate record of the research process and sources used;
- use a referencing system and bibliography and explain the importance of them.

2.1 Research sources

Where will you go for information on your chosen topic?

The following points can be made about your sources:

- use a range of different relevant sources;
- make sure the information is up-to-date;
- make sure your sources are sufficient to back up your findings and conclusions.

These are all **secondary** sources, but the nature of your dissertation may require you to do some field or **primary** research.

Primary research is a time-consuming process; if a questionnaire is to be used be very careful about the way in which questions are asked. Will you want to draw quantitative data from your questionnaire? This may require a tick box approach.

Qualitative or quantitative research?

Q1: Research the difference between qualitative or quantitative research.

School textbooks in Business Management are likely to cover this area in sufficient detail for your needs. In addition, there are business dictionaries available online.

A successful questionnaire

Q2: This activity is aimed only at those who expect to be designing a questionnaire or conducting a survey.

Research factors to remember when designing a successful questionnaire. Use the internet to find articles on this subject using the key words "questionnaire design".

2.1.1 Verifying sources of evidence

You should always try to judge whether your source can be trusted.

Newspapers often show a political bias, though it may not always be obvious. They may be "economical with the truth" presenting only those parts of the truth that suit their opinion. As elections approach, this bias is even greater. As a general rule, items in The Telegraph, may tend to favour political views on the right and The Guardian may favour more liberal-left views. The BBC news may be more impartial, but even it was heavily criticised in some quarters for its coverage of the Scottish referendum.

The print and television media mentioned in the previous paragraph are about as reliable as any, but you may need to look for another source to verify the "facts". It is important to use several sources and form a balanced opinion when researching.

The internet is no more reliable than the printed word. Wikipedia, for example, allows open access which means that some articles can be wrongly amended or inaccurate. Editors do check postings and remove errors, but this can take time. Therefore, always seek to confirm Wikipedia information by looking at other trusted websites.

The ONS (Office for National Statistics) is probably the best source for economic "facts" in the UK. However, like all state-run organisations, it may be influenced by government, if only indirectly through the selection of senior staff.

2.1.2 Plagiarism

A plagiarist is defined as: "someone who steals the thoughts or writings of others and presents them as his or her own". (Chambers, *The Chambers Dictionary*, 1998 edition, p1250)

The SQA definition is: "failing to acknowledge sources properly and/or submitting another person's work as if it were your own". (SQA, *Coursework Authenticity: A Guide for Teachers and Lecturers*, August 2009, p1)

Examples of plagiarism include:

- purchase of an essay from the internet;
- allowing another person to carry out the work that your name is on;
- failing to accurately identify sources used;
- copying sections of text (from friends, textbooks, internet, etc.) without acknowledging the source.

To avoid plagiarism:

- make notes from more than one source, understand the information, and then ***put it into your own words***;
- acknowledge the source of all quoted material;
- read and understand the latest version of the SQA booklet 'Your Coursework' (http://www.sqa.org.uk/sqa/71527.html) .

2.2 Project marking

Your project amounts to one third of your final mark and is marked out of 40.

The 40 initial marks are allocated specifically to six aspects as follows:

1. Introduction (3);
2. Analysis and evaluation (18);
3. Conclusions (6);
4. Research (4);
5. Structure and coherence (6);
6. Presentation and referencing (3).

You may notice that research is only allocated 4 marks, but the quality of your research will impact greatly on the rest of your project. Your research is the foundation of a good project and if your research is inadequate your project will not impress. The computing phrase, "garbage in garbage out" describes how poor research will lead you to erroneous conclusions.

Four marks will be awarded for research that strongly supports the economic case being put forward. At the other extreme, a failure to reference your research sources or the research being irrelevant or out-of-date would result in zero marks for research. This would also impact on marks elsewhere on the project which would be built without foundations.

2.3 Project introduction

Your project introduction should:

- state the aims of your project;
- identify clearly the economic issue;
- clarify and explain its significance to the wider economy.

You begin by stating clearly the "terms of reference" for your project. For additional credit you should expand and develop your aims to explain why your topic is a significant economic issue.

Your project should progress in a logical way with a coherent structure that leads naturally to your conclusions. You should include headings and subheadings that will assist the marker in following your line of reasoning. Ensure that any economic terms you use are accurate and properly explained.

Project introduction Go online 

The following text is an example of a project introduction.

"The Barnett Formula is a topical economic issue because its existence is currently being questioned. It provides for public expenditure made in England to be available to Scotland (and Wales and Northern Ireland) and enhances the amount available per person to these areas. This is often said to reflect the additional expense of providing services in regions where population density is low, and adds to the funds available in historically more deprived areas of the UK. The principal aim of the project is to establish whether there is still justification for having a Barnett Formula."

Q3: Outline the best parts of this introduction.

. . . .

Q4: Indicate what improvements could be made.

2.4 Project analysis and evaluation

These are your findings and this is the substantive section of your project with 18 marks at stake. Marks will be awarded for the overall quality and depth of your analysis. To gain marks you will need to:

- apply economic theory to explain your data and predict economic outcomes for individuals, firms, markets or the economy;
- assess critically the significance and quality of the data your research has provided;
- decide on which factors can be given most weight and justify these decisions;
- show an understanding of the limits of economic analysis, when applied to the real world;
- show awareness of alternative economic theories and explain alternative interpretations of the data if there are any.

Mistakes to be avoided include:

- only describing and failing to explain or analyse;
- wandering away from the stated aims into remarks that are irrelevant to the terms of reference that you established;
- missing opportunities to provide relevant graphs and tables that assist your analysis.

Project analysis and evaluation Go online 

The following text is a snippet from a project analysis.

"The Barnett Formula is a 1970s device that was itself an updated from the 1880s Goschen Formula.

When additional money is allocated to spending in England, then Scotland, Wales and Northern Ireland receive a share of that additional spending provided.

There is no requirement for the devolved ministries to spend this money in a particular way that mimics English spending.

Barnett should become less and less important. The new Scotland Bill, if passed, transfers income tax raising powers to Scotland. This means the Barnett Formula will be less significant.

If you believe it is outrageous for tax income produced in one part of the country to be spent across the whole of the UK then remember that North Sea oil and gas receipts - 90% of which come from Scottish waters - are shared across the country for the benefit of all. Revenue from Scottish oil has for three decades matched approximately the additional public spending per person in Scotland."

Q5: Outline the best parts of this analysis.

....

Q6: Indicate what improvements could be made.

2.5 Project conclusion

Your project conclusions:

- must avoid repetition of the earlier contents of the project;
- should be consistent with the aims stated at the start of the project;
- should follow naturally from your evaluation of the research data;
- might not be straightforward and may use probabilities and judgements based on the evidence.

Mistakes that are to be avoided include:

- your conclusions not matching up with the aims of the project which you set out at the start;
- your conclusions not following logically from your findings and analysis;
- repeating earlier analysis (marks are not generally given for saying the same thing twice so your conclusions should be worded in a summative way).

Project conclusion Go online 

The following text is an example of a single conclusion.

"If the Barnett Formula were discontinued, a mechanism to redistribute from more prosperous regions to less prosperous ones would still be required within a single nation state. An effective regional policy would have to be created in its place. Pockets of deprivation across the country would continue to receive additional resources. Areas of Glasgow and some other Scottish cities rank among the most deprived and therefore whatever scheme replaced Barnett would still see the transfer of additional public spending to these areas. It might however see some redistribution to areas such as north-east England where there is some of the highest unemployment."

Q7: Outline the best parts of this single conclusion.

....

Q8: Indicate what checks should be made on a conclusion.

2.6 Project structure and coherence

Your project structure should be set out in the following order:

1. Start with a front cover that includes your name, the title, and the word count.
2. Include a contents page, and check the final section numbering as it may alter as you progress.
3. Write an introduction outlining clearly the issue and the range of your project, justifying your choice of topic as current and economically significant. You will also refer to the research methods you will be using.
4. Write the main body of the project, divided by headings and, if required, subheadings.
5. Follow this with your conclusions based on the research in the previous section.
6. Include a bibliography.
7. Add any appendices (up to a maximum of three). Where possible, place diagrams next to the relevant text within the main body rather than as an appendix.

Project structure and coherence Go online

Place the following words in the appropriate sentences below:

- bibliography;
- conclusions;
- count;
- diagrams;
- economic;
- numbering;
- subheadings;
- three.

Q9: The front cover should indicate the word ....

....

Q10: After redrafting you will need to review the page .... on the contents page.

....

Q11: Your introduction should clearly justify your topic as both current and ....

....

Q12: Divide up the project with headings and ....

....

Q13: Your research will lead you directly to your ....

....

Q14: Note down your sources in a ....

....

Q15: Alongside relevant text place ....

....

Q16: The maximum number of appendices is ....

2.7 Project referencing and presentation

When referencing, the details to include, in brackets, following the quoted text are:

1. the title of the text or source material;
2. the name of the author (or editor);
3. the date of publishing or reprint;
4. the page number.

An example of a reference would be:

Chambers, *The Chambers Dictionary*, 1998 edition, p1250

As web sources are often updated frequently you must include the last date of access. For example the following quotation:

"an act or instance of using or closely imitating the language and thoughts of another author without authorization and the representation of that author's work as one's own."

would have the following website reference:

Dictionary.com (2015) *Plagiarism*[online], available from http://dictionary.reference.com/browse/plagiarism (accessed 13/12/15)

Here are some guidelines and good practice for presentation in your project:

- use a clear font/font size - e.g. Times New Roman, minimum point size is 12;
- double-line spacing makes it far easier on the reader (although one and a half line spacing may be an acceptable compromise between readability and economy of resources);
- margins of 25 mm (one inch) are appropriate;
- select helpful page breaks;
- number pages clearly and after edits and check they are as listed in the contents section;
- give full details of sources for any quotations or diagrams and complete a bibliography;
- place diagrams alongside relevant text.

2.8 Project bibliography

Keep a note as you go along of every relevant text and website that you read. These can be placed in alphabetical order (by author/editor/website title).

The bibliography goes at the end of your submission, for example: Heriot-Watt University, *Scholar Study Guide CfE Advanced Higher Business Management, Researching an economic issue* (2015); Hamilton, A. In this example I have decided that the editing organisation leads rather than the author - but it could just as well have led with the author's name.

Bibliography Go online

Q17: A check or judgement on truth or accuracy

a) Bibliography
b) Plagiarism
c) Referencing
d) Verification

....

Q18: A list of items referred to in the course of writing your project

a) Bibliography
b) Plagiarism
c) Referencing
d) Verification

....

Q19: Acknowledging the source of quoted material

a) Bibliography
b) Plagiarism
c) Referencing
d) Verification

....

Q20: Presenting another's writing as your own

a) Bibliography
b) Plagiarism
c) Referencing
d) Verification

2.9 Key points to consider when researching and writing your project

In summary, the key points to consider when researching and writing your project are:

- select a current issue that interests you and phrase it as a question;
- time management is important, so agree deadlines for the completion of sections of the task with your teacher and stick closely to them;
- research widely and maintain a bibliography. Watch out for developments that occur as you are writing as they may require changes to be made;
- refer closely to the way in which marks are allocated and present your project in a format that seeks to gather in these marks;
- follow the teacher's advice on layout and presentation;
- use economic theory to explain wherever possible;
- draw your conclusions from the evidence and explicitly state how the evidence leads you to your conclusions;
- the allocation of marks within the project has changed beginning session 2019-2020 so make certain you have been supplied with the up-to-date allocation of marks.

2.10 Summary

Summary

You should now be able to:

- develop independent research skills;
- understand the difference between qualitative and quantitative research;
- evaluate if the range of sources used is appropriate for the needs of the research;
- keep an accurate record of the research process and sources used;
- use a referencing system and bibliography and explain the importance of them.
- the allocation of marks within the project has changed beginning session 2019-2020 so make certain you have been supplied with the up-to-date allocation of marks.

2.11 End of topic test

End of Topic 2 test Go online

Q21: What does your project start with?

a) A front cover
b) A contents page
c) The introduction

....

Q22: Which of the following is a suitable font and font size?

a) Times New Roman, 10
b) Tahoma, 18
c) Arial, 12

....

Q23: Primary research might involve you in:

a) producing a questionnaire.
b) surfing the internet.
c) reading a newspaper.

....

Q24: An acceptable line spacing would be:

a) single.
b) double.
c) triple.

Place the following words in the appropriate sentences below:

- bibliography;
- conclusions;
- diagrams;
- time;
- up-to-date;
- word count.

Q25: .... management is important.

....

Q26: Research widely and maintain a ....

....

Q27: Make sure the information is ....

. . . .

Q28: Start with a front cover that includes your name, the title, and the ....

. . . .

Q29: Place .... alongside relevant text.

. . . .

Q30: Draw your .... from the evidence.

Unit 3 Topic 3

Researching an economic issue test

Researching an economic issue test Go online

For the following questions, choose all the answers that apply.

Q1: Your project will require:

a) good time management.
b) wide research that you record.
c) a descriptive approach.
d) frequent repetition of your analysis.

....

Q2: The project:

a) is worth a quarter of the total marks for this course.
b) must be on a topical economic issue.
c) should always include a questionnaire or survey.
d) should not exceed 4,000 words.

....

Q3: Your conclusions must:

a) include a bibliography.
b) follow logically from your findings and analysis.
c) match up with the aims set out at the start of the project.
d) avoid the detailed repetition of material presented earlier in the project.

....

Q4: Which of the following is neither required nor recommended?

a) Maintaining a bibliography
b) Noting the word count
c) Adding a graphic to the front cover
d) Placing diagrams alongside relevant text

....

Q5: Primary, qualitative research could involve:

a) interviewing individuals for your research and recording what they say.
b) going online to find any previous research that is relevant to you project.
c) issuing a questionnaire and tallying up the scores from the ticked boxes.
d) going to a library and looking at copies of old newspapers.

....

Q6: Analysing and evaluating your research will require:

a) assessing the source for reliability and possible bias.
b) ensuring that equal weight is attached to all aspects of your research.
c) the application of economic theory to the data.
d) occasionally wandering away from the stated aims to explore other areas.

....

Q7: Mistakes to be avoided in your project include:

a) missing opportunities to provide relevant graphs and tables.
b) having the word count displayed on the front cover.
c) producing a project that is merely descriptive.
d) placing diagrams alongside relevant text.

....

Q8: Which of the following subject titles would make the basis for a suitable project?

a) The Great Depression
b) Has inequality in the UK increased in recent years?
c) Why did house prices fall in 2008?
d) The meaning of globalisation

Glossary

Barriers to entry

make it difficult for a rival to enter a monopolised industry (e.g. economies of scale)

Bibliography

a list of works (or sources) referred to in the process of writing your dissertation

Branding

the use of a distinctive product name which can be backed up with marketing activity to create a brand identity (or image) in the consumers' minds

Collusion

agreements among firms that seek to avoid price wars and full competition and act against the interests of the consumers

Common Agricultural Policy

an expensive system of subsidies paid to European Union farmers

Competition and Markets Authority

an independent public body charged with ensuring healthy competition between companies for the benefit of companies, customers and the economy

Convergence

the need for an economy joining the single currency to match up with the economic indicators of existing eurozone members before joining

Demerit goods

can be provided by the market but in excessive numbers; the social costs are greater than the private costs

Deregulation

the removal of restrictions on business so that competition can be increased to encourage the efficient operation of markets

Developing economy

a nation with low GDP per capita and low levels for literacy and life expectancy

Duopoly

a specific type of oligopoly where two firms dominate a market, e.g. Coca Cola and Pepsi Cola

Economically inactive

not in the working population; neither in a job nor looking for one

Economic efficiency

more than just maximum output from minimum input (technical efficiency) because the goods and services produced must also be exactly what the consumers desire most as indicated by them in the market

Emerging economy

a nation going through a process of industrialisation and rapid growth which shares some of the features of an advanced economy, but is not yet an advanced economy

Enlargement

the widening of the European Union to include new members

Equilibrium output

this is the firm's profit-maximising output

Equilibrium price

a market clearing price at which demand equals supply

Euro

the single currency used by those EU members who have joined the eurozone

Eurozone

the name given to the group of EU countries that have adopted the euro as their currency

Externalities

costs (or benefits) that land on third parties who were not involved in the transaction between buyer and seller, e.g. pollution

Factor market

the market for a factor of production. For example, the market for labour has a demand for labour and a supply of labour. Where these two lines intersect is the wage rate (or price of labour)

Four-firm concentration ratio

a way of measuring the degree of oligopoly by adding up the market share of the largest four companies operating in an industry

Futures market

contract prices for the delivery and payment at some point in the future. These contracts can be traded, and the initial party to the contract may not be the one taking delivery. Certainty over future prices reduces risk and encourages companies to be involved on the futures market

Game theory

firms in oligopoly must assess the responses of competitors to any changes they make, e.g. prices, investment plans, before going ahead. Game theory seeks to develop a theory for this approach to decision-making

Globalisation

in Economics, it refers to increases in international trade, communications and investment leading to further economic integration and the increasingly free movement of goods, capital and labour in a global marketplace

Government intervention

the ways in which government can respond to market failure such as subsidies and taxation, for example

Government transfers

the movement of money from taxpayers to benefit recipients

Homogeneous product

identical products not differentiated by branding or packaging

Imperfect competition

includes every market type other than perfectly competitive markets

Income redistribution

the use of progressive taxes to take a higher percentage of income from the rich, for redistribution through government action or benefits to those on lower incomes

Kinked demand curve

in oligopoly an increase in price will lead to a large loss of customers to competitors but a cut in price is matched by rivals and few new customers are acquired. This leads to a kinked demand curve - price elastic for higher prices and price inelastic for lower prices

Life expectancy

the average number of years lived; life expectancy at birth can be considered a measure of the overall quality of life in a country

Literacy rates

the percentage of a population that can read and write at a given age; low levels of education hold back economic development

Long-run

a period of time that allows all the factors of production to be varied

Marginal cost pricing

this occurs where the market price just equals the marginal cost

Market failure

occurs when resources are allocated inefficiently by a free market, e.g. merit goods

Merit goods

can be provided by the market but not in sufficient numbers; the private benefits are less than the social benefits

Monopolistic competition

there are many suppliers of similar products who seek to differentiate their products from their competitors by finding a unique selling point

Monopoly

in theory there is only one firm in the industry, but in everyday usage it refers to a market that is dominated by one firm

Multinational

firms that have production units based in more than one country

Natural monopolies

a situation where the only efficient way to run an industry is with one firm

Non-price competition

competition on a variety of factors other than price, e.g. opening hours, loyalty cards, advertising

Normal profits

a return to enterprise that does not encourage entry to an industry but is sufficient to discourage exit

Oligopolistic competition

the form of competition that occurs in a market dominated by a few large firms

Oligopoly

a market dominated by a few large firms

OPEC (Organisation of the Petroleum Exporting Countries)

a group of major oil producers including Saudi Arabia, who act like a cartel and meet regularly to discuss production levels and prices. Norway, the UK and the USA are among oil producers who are not members

Perfect competition

a market with a large number of buyers and sellers, an homogeneous product, perfect knowledge and freedom of entry to and exit from the industry

Perfect knowledge

a requirement of perfect competition that regards buyers and sellers as being entirely aware of all aspects of the market place (e.g. prices in different locations)

Price leadership

a tendency in oligopolistic markets for firms to follow the pricing moves of the dominant firm. It can also be called tacit collusion

Price takers

firms operating in perfectly competitive markets are unable to influence the market price and are described as price takers

Price transparency

comparisons of prices in different countries are made easier for consumers through the use of a single currency

Primary research

new field research designed and carried out specifically for your project

Product differentiation

creating a unique selling point for your product by making it different in some respect from the potential substitutes

Profit maximisation (in monopoly)

occurs where marginal revenue equals marginal cost, and in the case of monopoly allows above normal profits that can be maintained in the long-run

Progressive tax

a tax that takes a higher percentage of income from the rich than from the poor

Public goods

goods which cannot be provided for a profit due to difficulties excluding non-payers, e.g. street-lighting

Public sector net borrowing

a measure of annual borrowing by government

Qualitative research

research that gives rise to subjective data such as opinions that can not easily be measured or aggregated

Quantitative research

research that gathers information in such a way that it may be measured and aggregated, often resulting in tables, graphs and predictions

Real GDP growth

an actual increase in the goods and services produced by a nation in a year (after allowing for the effects of inflation on prices)

Seasonally adjusted

statistics smoothed to remove regular annual changes that can cover up the overall trend, e.g. the temporary impact of school leavers in the summer on employment figures

Secondary research

desk research using material that has already been gathered for another (probably similar) purpose

Short-run

a period of time when at least one factor of production is a fixed cost

Single market

a new programme of policies adopted by the EU on 1 January 1993 which advanced beyond the mere abolition of trade barriers

Spot market

the price for immediate delivery of, and payment for, a commodity, e.g. oil. The spot market is sometimes called the "cash market"

Structural deficit

the level of the deficit exists when the economy is at full employment (not in recession), arising from infrastructure spending by government

Sub-normal profits

profits that are low enough to encourage firms to move resources to a different industry

Subsidies

payments made by government to encourage the production of goods and services and commonly used to encourage merit goods

Super-normal profits

profits that are sufficient to attract new firms into the industry

Tacit collusion

no contact between firms is needed - only a mutual understanding of the nature of oligopolistic competition. It is similar to price leadership

Taxation

the general raising of revenue by government, but often used to address market failure and discourage the overproduction of demerit goods and services

Hints for activities for Economic markets

Topic 3: Monopoly

Monopolist's cost and revenue table

Hint 1: Total Revenue = Output x Price (column 3); Profit = Total Revenue - Total Cost (column 5); Marginal Cost is the increase in Total Cost from making one additional unit (column 6); Marginal Revenue is the increase in Total Revenue from making and selling one additional unit (column 7); Average Total Cost is the Total cost divided by the number of units of output (column 8).

Hints to questions and activities for Researching an economic issue

Topic 1: How to organise your project

Selecting a topic

Hint 1:

- *The financial crisis of 2007-08 - should the banks have been saved?* This is now out of date.
- *Should the budget deficit be reduced?* This is a good question and current for a few years beyond 2016.
- *Should the UK join the euro?* This is not presently a current topic as the UK may be leaving the EU.
- *Why did house prices fall in 2008?* This is now out of date.
- *What were the causes of the Great Depression?* This is out of date as this is economic history.
- *What should be the favoured currency option if Scotland gained independence?* This is a good question, but check if it is acceptable given that a second referendum may never happen.
- *Is the UK heading for another recession?* This question should remain topical although the conclusion will vary over time.

Answers to questions and activities for Economic markets

Topic 1: Perfect competition

Market types (page 4)

Q1:

Monopolistic competition	Monopoly	Oligopoly	Perfect competition
making men's shirts	owning all the major UK airports	producing petrol	selling grade 1 King Edward potatoes
making women's shoes	producing a patented product	producing 'cola' soft drinks	selling medium size eggs
	running all buses in a local area		
	selling computer operating systems		

Perfectly competitive markets (page 6)

Q2: b) Homogeneous product

Q3: c) Freedom of entry and exit

Q4: d) Perfect knowledge

Q5: c) Freedom of entry and exit

Normal profit (page 9)

Q6: a) four

Q7: b) rent

Q8: c) interest

Q9: a) wages

Q10: c) profit

Q11: c) normal

Sub-normal profits (page 12)

Q12:

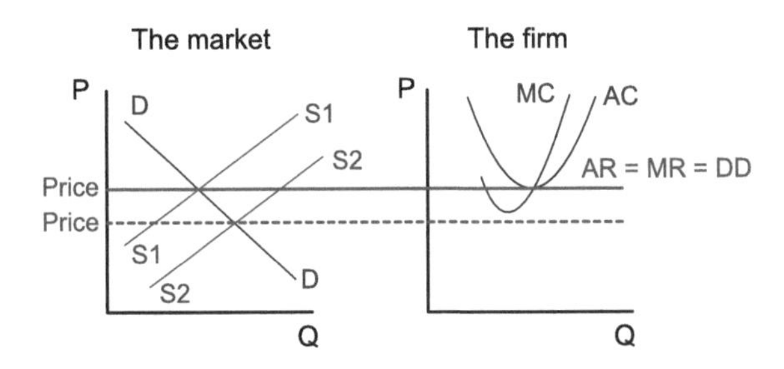

Q13: As the S1 line moves to the right to S2 in "the market" diagram, the horizontal red price line increases simultaneously following the intersection of D and S, as S1 rises to the new position of S2. At the higher price, normal profits are once again being made and the industry is back in equilibrium.

End of Topic 1 test (page 14)

Q14: b) super-normal profits

Q15: a) normal profits can be made.

Q16: c) Large economies of scale.

Q17: c) is one cost within the costs of production.

Q18: c) average variable cost.

Topic 2: Advantages and disadvantages of perfect competition

The conditions for perfect competition (page 19)

Q1:

True	False
Identical products	Few firms
Many buyers	Local monopoly
Many sellers	Price leaders
Normal profits	Price makers
Perfect knowledge	Product differentiation
Price takers	
Profit maximising	

Natural monopoly (page 21)

Q2: d) Railway tracks, electricity power lines and water pipes

Advantages and disadvantages of perfect competition (page 21)

Q3: a) Advantage

Q4: a) Advantage

Q5: b) Disadvantage

Q6: b) Disadvantage

Q7: a) Advantage

Fishing industry (page 23)

Q8: a) True

Q9: a) True

Q10: b) False

Q11: a) capital used cannot easily adapt to other uses.

Q12: c) neither enter nor exit the fishing industry.

Other markets in near perfect competition (page 24)

Q13: Your answer should focus on:

- the number of traders in the market;
- the knowledge traders have of other prices around the world for that currency or crop;
- whether traders are price takers and unable to influence the price;
- the extent to which the product is homogeneous.

End of Topic 2 test (page 25)

Q14: b) Price is equal to marginal price

Q15: d) fewer economies of scale.

Q16: c) the cost of labour, capital, rent and a normal profit.

Q17: a) Low prices

Q18: c) both of the above.

Q19: d) Competition reduces prices but limited funds for research.

Q20: With careful development, five ideas well explained would score 10 marks. Here are a number of scoring points that you should make in your answer:

1. The grocery market in the UK is dominated by a few large supermarket chains (e.g. Tesco, Morrisons, Sainsburys, Asda) and so is described as an oligopolistic market.
2. By reason of location the small grocer's shop may enjoy an element of local monopoly depending on the distance that needs to be travelled to get to alternatives. The convenience of the location stops the shop from being identical to its competitors.
3. Customers are often aware of the approximate prices of frequent purchases (e.g. milk) but there are many products they do not have perfect knowledge of (e.g. a specific bottle of wine).
4. Building a shop nearby to compete may be difficult due to planning regulations and raising the capital to do so may prove difficult. You would then have to overcome existing customer loyalty. Freedom of entry to the industry is thus curtailed.
5. The small shop is able to vary prices for products according to what its small local market will bear. The additional element of convenience makes its product different and it does not just accept prices from the market.

Topic 3: Monopoly

Monopolist demand curve (page 28)

Q1: b) The demand curve faced by a monopolist.

Q2: a) The demand curve faced by a firm in a perfectly competitive market.

Defining monopoly (page 29)

Q3: a) True

Q4: b) False

Q5: b) False

Q6: a) True

Barriers to entry (page 30)

Q7:

Terms	Descriptions
Licence	Mass producing low cost cars
Brand loyalty	Surveying, drilling, refining and retailing oil
Vertical integration	Low prices used to bankrupt competitor
Patents	Heinz Baked Beans in the shopping trolley every week
Predatory pricing	How Dyson stopped Hoover copying (for a while)
Economies of scale	Required to run a municipal taxi

Monopolist's cost and revenue table (page 33)

Q8:

Output units	Price (AR) per unit	TR (£)	TC (£)	Profit (£)	MC (£)	MR (£)	ATC (£)
0	100	0	50	-50	n/a	n/a	n/a
1	80	80	90	-10	40	80	90
2	75	150	120	30	30	70	60
3	70	210	144	66	24	60	48
4	65	260	160	100	16	50	40
5	60	300	180	120	20	40	36
6	55	330	210	120	30	30	35
7	50	350	259	91	49	20	37
8	45	360	312	48	53	10	39
9	40	360	369	-9	57	0	41
10	35	350	440	-90	71	-10	44

Cost and revenue diagram for a monopolist (page 33)

Q9:

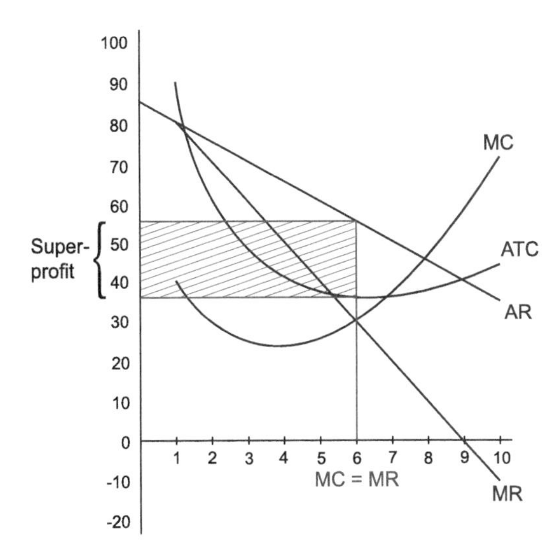

Disadvantages of a monopoly (page 34)

Q10:

Disadvantages of a monopoly
Economically inefficient
Higher prices
No choice
Slow innovation

The benefits of monopoly (page 35)

Q11: a) True

Q12: a) True

Q13: b) False

Q14: a) True

End of Topic 3 test (page 37)

Q15: a) Economies of scale

Q16: c) Marginal Cost = Marginal Revenue

Q17: c) both short-run and long-run super-profits.

Q18: b) economies of scale and vertical integration.

Q19: d) Prices are higher and barriers prevent new entrants to the market.

Q20: With careful development, five ideas well explained would acquire 10 out of 10 marks. Here are some scoring points that you should make in your answer:

1. A monopoly is dominated by one very large firm. Microsoft, with its Windows operating system, is such a company. In contrast there are a large number of smaller firms competing for sales in perfect competition.
2. Monopolists can set the price in the market, although consumers will then decide how much to buy at that price. Perfect competitors are price takers and are unable to influence the price set by the market forces of supply and demand.
3. In the short-run both a perfect competitor and a monopolist can achieve above-normal profits. The monopolist, thanks to barriers to entry into the market, can maintain above normal profits in the long-run. The perfect competitor will find new firms joining its industry and competing prices and profits down to a normal profit level in the long-run.
4. Economic efficiency is less under monopoly as the customer is paying more than the true cost of the goods, price is not equal to marginal cost, and the goods may be under-consumed. In perfect competition the equilibrium output of the firm is where price equals marginal cost and consumers cannot allocate their resources to better advantage.
5. Barriers to entry do not exist under perfect competition but a monopoly has many ways of excluding potential rivals, such as cutting prices below cost temporarily to drive them into bankruptcy.

Topic 4: Monopolistic competition

Characteristics of monopolistic competition (page 42)

Q1: b) False

Q2: a) True

Q3: b) False

Q4: b) False

Q5: a) True

Product differentiation in the footwear industry (page 44)

Q6: The following non-exhaustive list gives some examples of product differentiation in the footwear industry:

- men's / women's / unisex;
- half sizes available;
- shoes / trainers / boots / slippers;
- laces / slip-on / Velcro;
- materials - leather / artificial fibres;
- heel size;
- colour or combination of colours;
- shape;
- pattern / design on shoe;
- quality of lining;
- quality of exterior shoe;
- branding;
- display;
- advertising;
- availability in different outlets.

Product differentiation for oranges (page 44)

Expected answer

Your answer may include: price, packaging, shop location and ease of parking, quality control by retailer, ambience of shop, shelving and display, opening hours.

Product differentiation summary (page 44)

Q7: Product ***differentiation*** is a feature of monopolistic competition. A firm will create a ***brand*** with its own unique ***image***. However, many close ***substitutes*** will be available to consumers. Expenditure on ***advertising*** assists in creating consumer brand loyalty. This allows the firm some influence over ***price***. It makes the brand less price ***elastic***.

Advertising in monopolistic competition (page 45)

Q8:

Advantages of advertising	Disadvantages of advertising
Creates jobs	Adds to the cost of products
Increases economies of scale	Can be visual pollution
Informs potential customers of new products	Can mislead and fail to deliver the promised utility to buyers
Revenue funds media (e.g. television)	May detract from enjoyment of media (e.g. television)
	Tend to cancel each other out (adding to costs)

Making a loss (page 46)

Q9:

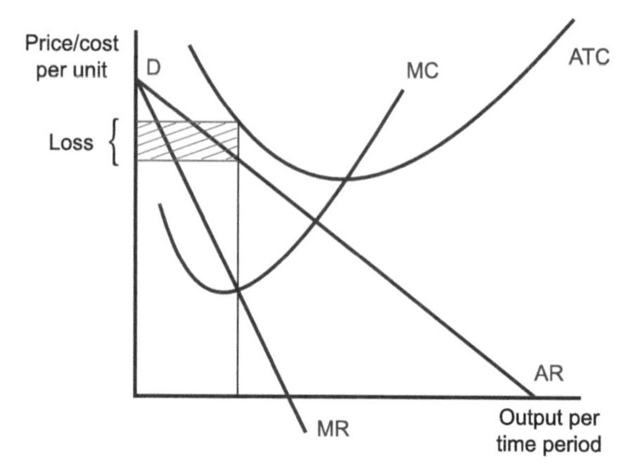

The loss-minimising point occurs where producing one more unit of output (the marginal unit) would give marginal revenue equal to the marginal cost of making it. Beyond this, the cost of making another unit would exceed the revenue returned - and losses would begin to increase.

Therefore the vertical line at output quantity Q, which runs through the intersection of MR and MC, is the key to the loss minimising of the firm in monopolistic competition. Continue this line upwards through the average revenue line to the average total cost curve.

Notice the two red-coloured horizontal lines leading to the vertical axis. The lower line marks the average revenue (price) and the upper line marks the average cost. The difference between them is the loss (or at least sub-normal profit) made by the firm in monopolistic competition per unit sold. Remember that a normal profit is included in the term average cost, and average revenue below average cost initially indicates sub-normal profit and then a loss.

Finally notice the rectangle within the boundaries of the red lines. This multiplies the loss (or sub-normal profit) per unit by the units of output to give a diagrammatic representation of losses at the loss minimising output level of Q.

End of Topic 4 test (page 48)

Q10: c) monopolistic competition.

Q11: d) the use of brand names, the use of packaging and variations in colour and style.

Q12: a) substitutes.

Q13: b) competitors can enter the market with close substitutes.

Q14: c) each firm has only a small share of the market.

Q15: With careful development, five ideas well explained would acquire 10 out of 10 marks. Here are some scoring points that you should make in your answer:

1. In monopolistic competition there are a large number of suppliers producing similar but differentiated products. For example, clothing in many different styles and fashions. In contrast there is an even greater number of small firms competing for sales in perfect competition producing identical products.
2. Monopolistic competitors have some control over the price of their product although the number of fairly close competitors will limit their pricing options. Perfect competitors are price takers and are unable to influence the price set by the market forces of supply and demand. They face a horizontal demand curve.
3. In the short-run both a perfect competitor and a monopolistic competitor can achieve above-normal profits. In both cases the entry of new firms into the industry is possible. This will result in the competing down of super-profits to normal profits, at which point entrepreneurs will cease to seek entry into the industry. However the firm in monopolistic competition has the advantages of branding and product differentiation so it has opportunities to re-establish above-normal profits.
4. Economic efficiency is less under monopolistic competition as the customer is paying more than the true cost of the goods. This could be considered a premium that the consumer is willing to pay for variety and choice in the market place. In perfect competition average total costs are at the minimum but for the monopolistic competitor the equilibrium output of the firm is to the left of the minimum point on the average cost curve where price is greater than marginal cost. Consumers could allocate their resources to better advantage.
5. Barriers to entry do not exist under either perfect competition or monopolistic competition. However, the monopolistic competitor can attempt to stay ahead of rivals by using marketing and design to create a differentiated product with consumer brand loyalty. These options are not available under conditions of perfect competition.

Topic 5: Oligopoly

Types of market structure (page 50)

Q1:

Number of sellers	Market structure
one	monopoly
two	duopoly
few	oligopoly
many	monopolistic competition
unlimited	perfect competition

Characteristics of oligopolistic markets (page 51)

Q2: b) False

Q3: a) True

Q4: a) True

Q5: a) True

Q6: b) False

Q7: a) True

Brands operating in oligopolistic markets (page 54)

Q8:

Aircraft manufacture	Boeing and Airbus
Soft drink manufacture	PepsiCo and The Coca-Cola Company
Consumer goods	Procter & Gamble and Unilever
Computer systems	Apple and Microsoft

Q9:

Automotive industry	BMW, Daimler AG, Fiat, Ford, General Motors, Hyundai, Nissan, PSA Peugeot Citroën, Renault, Toyota, Volkswagen
Banking	Barclays, HSBC, Lloyds Banking Group, RBS
Fast food restaurants	Burger King, KFC, McDonald's
DIY stores	B&Q, Focus, Homebase
Supermarkets	Asda, Morrisons, Sainsburys, Tesco

Non-price competition (page 56)

Q10: The following non-exhaustive list gives some examples of ways in which oligopolistic firms may compete without resorting to price cuts:

- loyalty cards;
- television advertising;
- money-off tokens in newspapers;
- home delivery;
- cheap petrol including money-off for store purchases over £50;
- extended opening hours e.g. 24 hours;
- internet catalogue and sales;
- new technology - self-scanning at till;
- provision of other services - e.g. optician, post office, credit cards, insurance.

End of Topic 5 test (page 61)

Q11: An oligopolistic market is dominated by ***5*** firms. They produce ***differentiated*** products. ***Non-price*** competition is the typical form of competition. Expenditure on advertising is often ***large***. The largest four firms could share ***50%*** of the market. The largest firm may offer price ***leadership***. Any price increase is likely to result in a price ***elastic*** response because other firms hold their prices. This reactive behaviour is termed ***game*** theory.

Q12: Your answer needs to cover the following:

1. The kinked demand curve with an explanation of the disadvantages of competing by lowering your price and the effect on profits.
2. Examples of the ways in which non-price competition takes place. UK supermarkets provide plenty of examples of these, e.g. advertising, loyalty cards, cheap petrol.
3. An outline of game theory, i.e. the idea that these firms must constantly assess the next moves of their competitors and consider the responses of competitors to any decisions they make.

Topic 6: Market failure

Market failure (page 64)

Q1: The following four points could be made:

- markets that fail to function efficiently in the way they price or allocate goods;
- the private business sector of the economy cannot supply some goods and services;
- the market works to an extent but the goods and services are priced too low or too high and the wrong quantities are produced;
- the market may not provide goods in a fair (or equitable) way, leading to extremes of wealth and poverty.

To answer this question fully, you should back up these points with suitable examples from your own internet research.

Street lighting (page 65)

Q2: A feature of public goods (and services) is that when a person makes use of them, they do not buy them and place them under private ownership, which would diminish their quantity and deny the next person the ability to use them. Public goods are therefore non-diminishable as well as non-excludable, and Sophie's use of the lights in no way uses them up or detracts from their availability to the next person.

Demerit goods (page 66)

Q3: Demerit goods can be provided by the market, but in excessive numbers. The social costs are greater than the private costs. This can be shown diagrammatically.

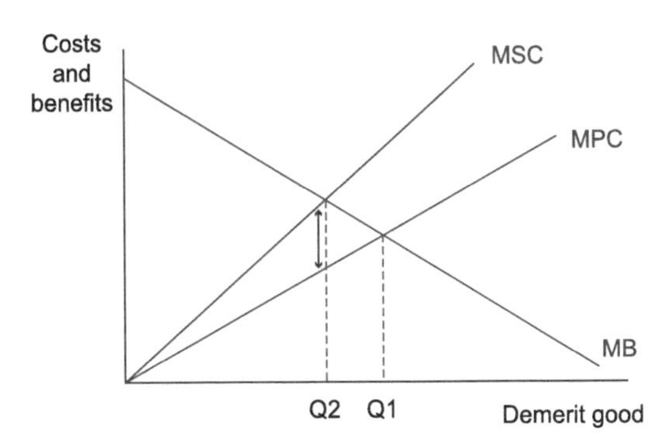

Marginal social costs (MSC) compared with marginal private costs (MPC) for a demerit good

This diagram shows that marginal social costs (MSC) exceed marginal private costs (MPC) for a demerit good such as whisky. The arrowed gap between marginal social costs and marginal private costs represents the marginal external (third party) costs. While whisky creates private costs reflected in the market price before taxation it also creates social costs.

One example of a wider social cost may be the cost to the general taxpayers of dealing with increased levels of drunkenness and illness. These costs may fall on publically funded services such as police, social work and health care. Thus a demerit good has wider costs for society beyond the private costs. If it was available in a free market without government taxation, age restriction, and licensing of shops and premises, then Q1 of whisky would be consumed.

Demerit goods are over-consumed in this marketplace. The efficient use of scarce resources would involve a lower level of consumption at Q2 where the marginal benefit (MB) equals the entire marginal social cost and not just the cost to the private purchaser. Private customers would pay to consume whisky all the way to the point where the perceived marginal benefit equalled the marginal private costs. This would have unfortunate social costs. There is a strong case for the state to tax and restrict whisky to reflect the marginal social costs ensuring the allocation of valuable scarce resources to best advantage, taking into account the external third party costs.

Negative externalities (page 66)

Q4: Possible negative externalities associated with drinking alcohol:

- illness and health spending funded by taxpayers;
- noise and disturbance affecting the quality of life (and sleep) of other people;
- criminal behaviour in streets and associated police and legal costs funded by the taxpayer;
- additional car accidents resulting in injuries and deaths to third parties and costs;
- social and economic impact on family and relatives.

Q5: Possible negative externalities associated with driving gas-guzzling SUVs:

- environmental cost of running unnecessarily fuel inefficient vehicle (unless using fields and farm tracks regularly);
- wider parking spaces required, so fewer spaces available overall.

Q6: Possible negative externalities associated with smoking tobacco:

- increased health spending funded by taxpayers;
- passive third-party smoking (reduced recently by bans on smoking in public premises);
- costs to business of increased illness;
- fewer luxuries (e.g. holidays) for families as addict spends first on addiction.

Q7: Possible negative externalities associated with tarring over your front garden:

- increased risk of flooding for third parties arising from diversion of rain into drains, rather than soaking into ground;
- diminished quality of life for passers-by who might have seen a pretty garden.

Smoking - a merit or demerit good? (page 67)

Q8: This is a strange argument based on smokers contributing more to the exchequer than they use. This implies an overall third party gain. However remember that if smoking was not taxed the social costs presumably would outweigh the private benefits. Smoking is therefore a demerit good.

However, the case could be made for reducing taxation on tobacco if the taxation is so high as to create the anomaly that smokers contribute more to the community's welfare than the they use up. (A separate issue is that the tax on smoking is also regressive.)

This is all calculated on the basis of money changing hands. As an economist you will hopefully be having thoughts about the quality of life enjoyed by addicted smokers. One issue is whether addicts are able to make rational economic choices or their addiction affects their spending patterns in a way that detracts from their quality of life and that of their family. The third party social costs of smoke in cinemas, pubs, etc. have been reduced to zero recently. Perhaps this restriction on where people can smoke could be reflected by a reduction in taxation, as total negative externalities have reduced?

Barriers to entry (page 69)

Q9: *One possible solution is outlined below.*

The Windows operating system has become a standard, with the majority of the world's computers using it. Training is generally carried out on this system and operators around the world are familiar with it. Effectively it has become a universal standard, rather like VHS became for video cassette recorders or the standard track width became for railways. The consumer default is to purchase the familiar standard system as there will be far less software able to operate on non-standard products.

As an established brand and market leader, consumers will be reassured as to the quality of their products and importantly in computing with the compatibility of software purchases with their expensive hardware. With less familiar or new brands, consumers will have questions about compatibility or may simply choose not to purchase through a lack of knowledge of the new brand's capabilities and reliability.

As a wide-ranging company in the ICT business, Microsoft has developed horizontally and vertically to the point where it is a major influence in the market for many aspects of the supply of ICT. This may act as a constraint on other companies. They may have to negotiate contracts with Microsoft in order to advance. The attachment of Internet Explorer to other Microsoft purchases shows how a powerful firm in the market can seek to further widen its influence in ways not always open to competitors.

Economies of scale will enable Microsoft to cut costs and maintain prices in the market place that make it difficult for new firms to match. Marketing economies of scale will have given the brand and its logo worldwide recognition similar to that enjoyed by iconic brands such as Coca Cola. These benefits of size are not available to market newcomers, who thus face an uphill battle to establish themselves.

High profits will enable Microsoft to invest heavily in research and development (R&D). This should allow it to stay ahead of prospective competitors. It will quite possibly continue to innovate ahead of other firms due to the advantage given by its investment in R&D.

Regional unemployment (page 70)

Q10: In the 1980s your figures should show high rates of unemployment especially in North-West England, North-East England, Northern Ireland, Wales and Scotland. These areas were hardest hit by declining manufacturing and coal mining jobs and the associated negative multiplier effects on the local communities. Watching the film 'Pride' (2014) could give you an impression of this era. Similarly, the BBC's 'Andrew Marr's History of Modern Britain' deals with this era.

End of Topic 6 test (page 71)

Q11: b) allocate goods efficiently through the price mechanism.

Q12: b) the inability to exclude non-payers and the unlimited availability for use by others.

Q13: d) fewer road accidents, less congestion and less pollution.

Q14: a) profit.

Q15: a) Street lighting, education, alcohol

Q16: b) subsidise the relocation of unemployed workers and improve knowledge of vacancies.

Q17: c) third party costs (or benefits) that fall on neither the buyer nor the seller.

Q18: b) subsidised by government.

Q19: d) Radioactive particles from nuclear power plant on a public beach, the noise from a "hen" party going home at 2am and the dominance of Sky TV in bidding for live football.

Q20: a) For merit goods, the social benefits exceed the private benefits.

Q21: Approach this by dealing with each aspect separately and explaining examples. For example, using public goods, your answer may be similar to the following.

Public goods cannot be supplied by private entrepreneurs seeking a commercial profit, so the market would fail to provide them. *(1 mark)* The nature of public goods makes it impossible to fence them off from non-payers. *(1 mark)* If you can use the good without paying many would not pay. These "free riders" are the main problem with public goods - that is the non-excludability of non-payers. *(1 mark)* Examples include street lighting, public parks, lighthouses, fire brigades, police services and, perhaps, roads. *(1 mark)* Perhaps roads, because toll roads do exist, and the latest congestion charging technology opens up new charging possibilities.

Another feature of public goods is that using them does not usually diminish the quantity of that public good available to someone else. If you make use of a lighthouse, then in no sense is it diminished for another ship. *(1 mark)* You have not taken ownership of the lighthouse and hence denied or diminished its use by rivals. *(1 mark)* Public goods, if they are to be satisfactorily produced, need to be provided by central or local government using taxpayers' money. *(1 mark)*

Take a similar approach to merit goods, demerit goods and monopoly to complete your answer.

Topic 7: Government intervention

Adam Smith's concept (page 74)

Q1: In your answer you should refer to the following sections of "The Wealth of Nations":

> "[He who] intends only his own gain is led by an invisible hand to promote an end which was no part of his intention. Nor is it always the worse for society that it was no part of it. By pursuing his own interest [an individual] frequently promotes that of the society more effectually than when he really intends to promote it. I have never known much good done by those who affected to trade for the [common] good."

Smith also said:

> "It is not from the benevolence of the butcher, the brewer or the baker, that we expect our dinner, but from their regard to their own self interest. We address ourselves, not to their humanity but to their self-love, and never talk to them of our own necessities but of their advantages."

It is clear that Smith saw markets made up of independent sellers looking to profit as a very effective way of ensuring that the appropriate goods and services were provided for consumers. The self interest (or profit motive) ensured a rapid response to changing consumer demand. He clearly saw that decisions made in a decentralised way by thousands of individual buyers and sellers could be efficient in allocating resources.

Note: Right-wing (conservative, free market) politicians and economists are prone to quoting selectively from Adam Smith in support of free market theory. However, much of Adam Smith's tone elsewhere shows great concern for the less well-off in society, and despite his clear exposition of the advantages of markets, it seems likely he would have been well content with a degree of government intervention.

Economic intervention (page 75)

Expected answer

Here are some aspects of economic intervention that you may have on your own list:

- taxes;
- minimum wage laws (e.g. UK minimum wage);
- import quotas;
- tariffs;
- subsidies (e.g. EU sugar subsidies);
- production quotas (e.g. EU fish quotas);
- price limits;
- price support (e.g. Common Agricultural Policy of EU);
- licenses required;
- minimum age requirements;
- location and planning permission restrictions;

- opening hours restricted;
- social security;
- free health care provision;
- free state education.

Income redistribution (page 77)

Q2: Your reasons could include contagious illnesses, increased crime, increased risk of riots or violent revolution.

UK income tax (page 78)

Q3: The current answer can be obtained at https://www.gov.uk/income-tax-rates. Using the February 2015 figures (above) people start paying tax at £10,000 per annum. The higher rate is paid on every pound earned above £41,865. The additional rate applies to those earning over £150,000 per year who start paying 45% on every additional pound. These bands change every year, so obtain the latest figures on the web.

Q4: In 1974 the top-rate of income tax increased to 83%. It applied to incomes over £20,000, and because there was also a 15% surcharge on 'un-earned' income (investments, dividends) this could result in a 98% marginal rate of personal income tax. 750,000 people were eligible to pay top-rate income tax.

Q5: Depending on the success of your research you may have many different answers. Here are some of mine:

- In Germany the top rate for personal income tax rate for the highest earners is 45%.
- In Sweden the highest rate of personal income tax was 61%.
- In USA the highest rate of federal tax for personal income is 40%.

Provision of public goods (page 79)

Q6:

Government	Private	Partly private
Police	Cars	Education
Roads	Electricity	Health Services
Streetlights	Keep fit classes	Refuse collection
	School cleaning	Water

Some explanations for these answers:

- Cars: Provided by the private sector.
- Education: Available privately but delivered mainly by the state.
- Electricity: Supplied by private companies.
- Health services: Available privately but delivered mainly by the state.
- Keep fit classes: Provided by the private sector.
- Police: State provided although private security is available as well.
- Refuse collection: Often provided by local councils but can be outsourced.
- Roads: Toll roads remain quite rare.
- School cleaning: Mainly contracted out to private firms.
- Streetlights: Generally only supplied by government.
- Water: Privatised in England and Wales but supplied by the public sector in Scotland.

Q7: Until technology is able to monitor car use per mile and charge (as in congestion charging) ***roads*** are a good example of a public good, unless they are toll roads. It can though be argued that fuel tax and vehicle excise duty make users pay for some of the costs, and non-users do not pay these.

Streetlights can be classed as a public good. It is difficult to imagine people carrying technology that allows them to be charged on the basis of how many streetlights they walk or drive past.

Basic ***police*** services can be classed as a public good. Although they can be supplemented by paying for private security, the standard service cannot be delivered to one person without other non-payers positively benefiting. Where a particular event, such as a football match, occurs, the user (club and hence spectators in their admission fee) can be asked to pay.

Water and electricity meters are available so these industries should not be viewed as public goods because the user can be made to pay. A case can be made for them being natural monopolies, and the state may decide to deliver these services for that reason.

Whatever method of meeting the costs is used for education, health, and refuse collection, it remains that individuals can go private, e.g. the use of a rented skip for refuse collection. They are subsidised merit goods rather than public goods.

Answers from page 80.

Q8: Possible answers include:

- licences required to sell alcohol;
- age restrictions on sale of alcohol and cigarettes.

Q9: Possible answers include:

- illegal drugs;
- high calibre handguns.

Positive and negative externalities (page 80)

Q10:

Positive externalities	Negative externalities	Both positive and negative externalities
Keeping your front garden neat	Driving at 100mph	Decorating the outside of your house with 2,000 flashing lights at Christmas
Vaccinating your child against measles	Partying in the street at 3am	
	Smoking cigarettes	

Current levels of taxation (page 81)

Q11: Your research should give you the current levels of tax. As of February 2015:

- a £5 bottle of wine (13% alcohol) would be taxed with VAT 20% and duty 40%. The total tax would be £2.83 or 57% of the price.
- fuel duty and VAT was 58p per litre for petrol and diesel, half the price at the pump;
- an average price for 20 cigarettes in February 2015 was £8.47. The tax and duty totalled £6.49 which is 77% of the retail price.

Subsidies (page 82)

Q12:

Subsidised	Not subsidised
Education	Diesel cars
Eye tests	Newspapers
Medicines	
Museums	
Orchestras	
Rail travel	
Rural bus routes	
Sugar	

Here are some explanations for these answers:

- Education: Free for pupils in the state system.
- Eye tests: Free eye tests so the government pays.
- Medicines: Standard rate for prescriptions even if medicines are expensive.
- Museums: Any money made is not enough to cover all costs.
- Orchestras: Often subsidised, arguably a regressive subsidy for the middle classes.
- Rail travel: Railways receive government funds.
- Rural bus routes: Often awarded to the company requiring the least subsidy.
- Sugar: EU sugar subsidy to farmers.

Answers from page 83.

Q13: Monopoly leads to a misallocation of resources because the price signal fails to reflect the true costs of production and the good is likely to be under-consumed.

Regulatory bodies (page 86)

Expected answer

Ofwat is the body responsible for economic regulation of the privatised water and sewerage industry in England and Wales.

ORR is a statutory board which is the combined economic and safety regulatory authority for Great Britain's railway network.

Ofcom is the government-approved regulatory and competition authority for the broadcasting, telecommunications and postal industries of the United Kingdom.

End of Topic 7 test (page 87)

Q14:

Description	Government intervention
Checks on market domination	CMA
Discourage demerit goods	Taxes and duties
Encourage merit goods	Subsidies
Monitors prices and services	Regulatory bodies
Redistribute income	Progressive taxes
Required to operate	Licences

Q15: Externalities are the costs of economic activity borne by third parties not involved in the transaction as buyer or seller and therefore not reflected in the price charged. Internal costs are met by the seller who incurs them in the production process and passes these costs on to the purchaser in the price charged.

Q16: The planning system considers applications to build with a view to minimising externalities. It does this by restricting building in the countryside or where the amenity to third parties is adversely affected by the proposals. Planning authorities may suggest amendments to building plans or refuse applications altogether. This reduces external costs.

Q17: Measures should include:

- the role of the CMA (Competition and Markets Authority);
- the role of regulatory authorities;
- deregulation of markets.

In discussing effectiveness you should explain that:

- there remain many examples of oligopoly and, despite investigation by the CMA, they continue to flourish in some areas (e.g. buses);
- there are many examples of restrictions being placed on mergers and takeovers by the CMA;
- prices have been restricted by regulators;
- deregulation and "contracting out" encourage competition and can result in lower prices for customers - although in some cases low prices can be associated with lower quality (e.g. school cleaning);
- competition policies are not always applied. International markets may necessitate that the UK firm has a large UK market share and is very large in order to compete effectively worldwide.

Topic 8: Economic markets tests

Economic markets test (page 90)

Q1:

Description	Government intervention
A well-kept garden	Positive externality
Dominated by a few large firms	Oligopoly
Non-payers cannot be excluded	Public good
Only one firm in this industry	Monopoly
Over-provided by the market	Demerit good
Pollution from a factory chimney	Negative externality
Products differentiated by design and colour	Monopolistic competition
Taxes, subsidies and licences	Government intervention
Thousands of sellers of homogeneous product	Perfect competition
Under-provided by the market	Merit good

Q2: The following five areas, if suitably extended with examples, would provide a detailed answer to this question:

- ***Externalities*** - markets that fail to function efficiently in the way they price or allocate goods;
- ***Public goods*** (non-excludability of non-payers) - the private business sector of the economy cannot supply some goods and services;
- ***Merit goods and demerit goods*** - the market works to an extent but the goods and services are priced too low or too high and the wrong quantities are produced;
- ***Inequity*** - the market may not provide goods in a fair (or equitable) way, leading to extremes of wealth and poverty;
- ***Recession*** - market economies tend to experience cycles of expansion (booms) and contraction (recessions).

Q3: Demerit goods can be provided by the market, but in excessive numbers. The social costs are greater than the private costs. This can be shown in the diagram below.

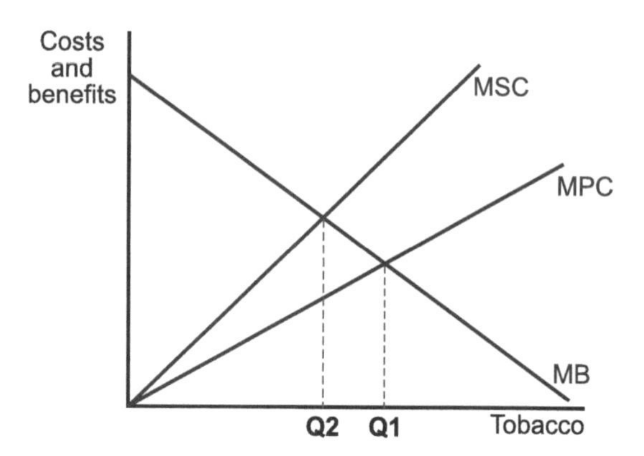

This diagram shows that marginal social costs (MSC) exceed marginal private costs (MPC) for a demerit good such as tobacco. The gap between marginal social costs and marginal private costs represents the marginal external (third party) costs. While tobacco creates private costs reflected in the market price before taxation it also creates social costs. One example of a wider social cost may be the cost to the general taxpayers of dealing with increased levels of illness. Another may be the reduction in the quality of the air in bars, cinemas and restaurants. These costs fall on the wider public. Thus a demerit good has wider costs for society beyond the private costs.

If it was available in a free market without government taxation and age restriction, then Q1 of tobacco would be consumed. Demerit goods are over-consumed in this marketplace. The efficient use of scarce resources would involve a lower level of consumption at Q2 where the marginal benefits equal the entire marginal social cost and not just the cost to the private purchaser. Private customers would pay to consume tobacco all the way to the point where the perceived marginal benefit equalled the marginal private costs. This would have unfortunate social costs.

There is a strong case for the state to tax and restrict tobacco to reflect the marginal social costs ensuring the allocation of valuable scarce resources to best advantage, taking into account the external third party costs.

Q4: With careful development, five ideas well explained would acquire 15 out of 15. Here are a number of scoring points that you should make in your answer:

1. Hairdressers all offer a service that is different in some way from that of their rivals. If it were perfect competition then the skill of the hairdressers, the decor of the premises and even the quality of the conversation would all have to be broadly equivalent in all hairdressers. This is clearly not the case.
2. By reason of location, the hairdresser may enjoy an element of local monopoly depending on the distance that needs to be travelled to get to alternatives. The convenience of the location also stops the shop from being identical to its competitors.
3. Customers are often aware of the approximate prices of frequent purchases but there are many services where they do not have perfect knowledge of all prices in the market. They may not be aware of the price structures offered by all the competitors. This is a lack of perfect knowledge and, again, the hairdresser does not fit the model for perfect competition.
4. Overcoming existing customer loyalty may make it difficult for a new hairdresser to establish successfully. This is a barrier to entry and in perfect competition there can be no barriers to entry. At least the capital costs of establishing are relatively small and that does indicate a similarity in one respect with perfect competition.
5. The small hairdresser is able to vary prices for products according to what its small local market will bear. The additional element of location makes its product different and it does not just accept prices from the market. On both these counts it is not a perfect competitor.

The market of the hairdresser is monopolistic competition and not perfect competition. It is typical of the majority of markets, in that each firm offers a slightly different proposition to customers.

Q5: Monopoly is technically inefficient - average total costs may not be at their lowest level.

Monopoly is allocatively inefficient - price is above marginal cost and the price level will be higher and the output lower than in more competitive markets.

The diagram below shows that, at the profit maximising point, monopolies do not produce at lowest average total cost. Price is also above marginal cost.

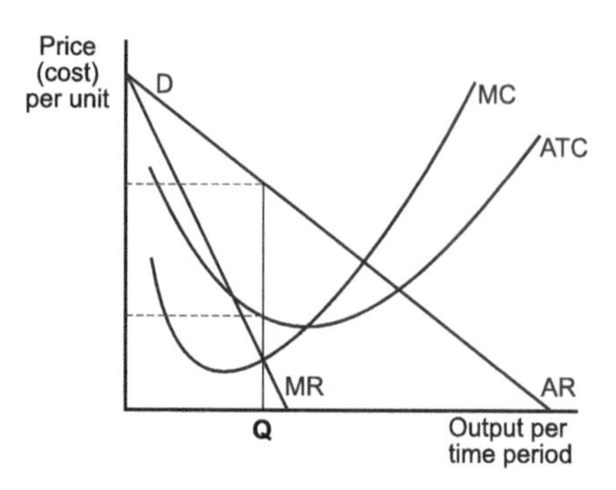

The profit maximising point occurs where producing one more unit of output (the marginal unit) would give marginal revenue equal to the marginal cost of making it. Beyond this, the cost of making another unit would exceed the revenue returned and, therefore, profits would begin to reduce.

The vertical line at output quantity Q, which runs through the intersection of MR and MC, is the key to the profit maximising of the monopolist. Continue this line upwards through the average total cost curve until it hits the average revenue (or market demand) line.

If there are barriers to entry these super-profits can be maintained in the long-run because no competitors will enter the market and compete prices and profits downwards. Therefore, we have now established the short-run and long-run equilibrium of a profit maximising monopolist.

In the diagram below we see that a monopoly uses its market power to restrict output to Q2 and to increase its price to P2. In a competitive market, the price would fall to P1 at quantity Q1. The high cost of production, as a result of the monopoly, causes under-consumption of the good and the misallocation of resources.

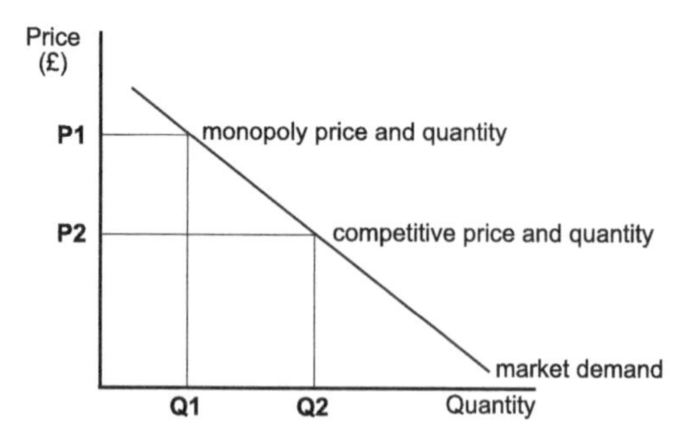

Answers to questions and activities for National and global economic issues

Topic 1: Recent trends in the national economy

GDP (page 96)

Q1: A guide answer for this question is not included as it will quickly become out of date.

Q2: A guide answer for this question is not included as it will quickly become out of date.

Inflation (page 97)

Q3: A guide answer for this question is not included as it will quickly become out of date.

Q4: A guide answer for this question is not included as it will quickly become out of date.

Unemployment trends (page 98)

Q5: The economy has returned to growth and is creating jobs during the business up-turn. Measures have been put in place to make it harder to claim benefits, and many benefits have fallen behind inflation. Wage growth has remained low (and often negative in real terms). Many workers gain employment on zero-hours contracts. Employers are therefore willing to hire labour as wage inflation is not a problem and business is improving. They are also able to remain flexible with their use of labour, due to zero-hours contracts.

Q6: The rise in employment rates must be linked to recent economic growth. It may also be due partly to the reduced level of benefits.

Q7: Three noteworthy transfers of public sector companies to the private sector contributed greatly to the trend. It has also been a period of job reduction in the public sector generally. For example, councils in England have shed a significant number of jobs over this period. The aim of reducing the budget deficit has been one cause, but it could also be partly motivated by the political persuasion of the governing party.

Q8: Real earnings were falling over several years. This reflects the lack of bargaining power of trade unions and individual workers in a deep recession. Job security became the primary concern, not increased earnings.

Q9: Economic inactivity will fall due to people joining the labour market. This is probably due to long-term social changes. Historically a main component would be the increasing number of married women in the labour force. Recent changes might be the result of improved state-provided child care, or an increase in the retirement age. Recent immigrants have a remarkably high participation in the labour market and that would also reduce the overall percentage inactive. Attempts by government to encourage some with disabilities back into work may also be a factor.

Q10: A guide answer for this question is not included as it will quickly become out of date.

Q11: A guide answer for this question is not included as it will quickly become out of date.

The budget deficit (page 102)

Q12: If the budget were always to be balanced, the government would not be using budget deficits and surpluses to influence the economy. This author would be against balanced budgets as it gives up an economic lever. The metaphor might be that you take a useful club (or tool for economic management) out of your golf bag (economic policy options).

Fiscal policy is an important tool of economic management and even after the elimination of a "structural deficit", it will still be useful to run a budget deficit or surplus to assist in achieving economic aims. The deficit should be measured against GDP, and its significance is reducing as it becomes a smaller proportion of GDP.

The level of interest rates paid on government borrowing (exceptionally low in recent years) is also important when assessing the impact of the deficit.

The exchange rate (page 103)

Q13: The US dollar.

Q14: A guide answer for this question is not included as it will quickly become out of date.

Q15: A guide answer for this question is not included as it will quickly become out of date.

The balance of payments (page 103)

Q16: The value of the pound has increased 10% against the euro since the beginning of the year. This held back the UK's exports in the first three months of the year, which were down £2.7bn on the previous quarter.

Q17: A guide answer for this question is not included as it will quickly become out of date.

Q18: A guide answer for this question is not included as it will quickly become out of date.

House prices (page 104)

Q19: A guide answer for this question is not included as it will quickly become out of date.

Q20: A guide answer for this question is not included as it will quickly become out of date.

Oil prices (page 105)

Q21: Demand factors: the coldness of a northern winter; the development of substitutes; more efficient cars; changing pollution laws; boom or recession.

Supply factors: political instability; supply decisions by OPEC cartel; major incidents such as refinery fires; the short term limits of storage containers.

Q22: A guide answer for this question is not included as it will quickly become out of date.

Q23: A guide answer for this question is not included as it will quickly become out of date.

Topic 2: Controlling the budget deficit and the national debt

Budget deficit reasons (page 108)

Q1: c) Recession

Q2: b) The structural deficit

Q3: a) Fiscal policy

Q4: d) Interest payments

Government borrowing (page 109)

Q5: During recessions, government spending in areas such as welfare increase but at the same time tax revenues reduce because personal and corporate incomes fall. Government also borrows for infrastructure projects and to increase spending in areas such as the NHS.

Sale of public sector assets (page 110)

Q6: In the case of Royal Mail, taking on the pension fund gave government a windfall for one year. However in the longer term, considerable liabilities for future pensions will have to be met. This means the overall effect on the public finances is unlikely to be beneficial. Assets could generate income for many years ahead if retained and run efficiently.

National debt comparison (page 112)

Q7: Belgium, Cyprus, France, Greece, Ireland, Italy, Portugal, Spain.

Q8: No solution is available as this will change over time.

Q9: No solution is available as this will change over time.

Q10: No solution is available as this will change over time.

Recent trends in UK government borrowing (page 113)

Q11: Borrowing increased from 2000 onwards peaking in 2009-10 at over £150 billion in the aftermath of the banking collapse and with the public ownership of several rescued banks. Since then it has declined gradually to under £90 billion.

Budget deficit forecast figures (page 114)

Q12: No solution is available as this will change over time.

Reliability of sources (page 115)

Q13: Sources quoted come from opposition political figures and cannot be regarded as neutral. Even if the figures produced by politicians are accurate, they may well have been selectively chosen to promote the argument that they are making. Therefore a researcher should seek to check these figures against other sources.

City analysts pointed out that income tax receipts were weak and have made deficit forecasts hard to reach.

Despite a drop in unemployment, income tax receipts are low because so many of the jobs created are low wage jobs.

End of Topic 2 test (page 116)

Q14: b) Higher rates of economic growth

Q15: b) 2009-10

Q16: c) long-term investment in infrastructure by government.

Q17: d) led to falls in UK net borrowing as a percentage of GDP.

Topic 3: Trends in the Scottish oil industry

Licensing round (page 118)

Q1: The Oil and Gas authority awarded 41 new licences for oil and gas operations in the North Sea, bringing the latest licensing round to a total of 175 licences covering 353 blocks. (Source: the Press and Journal, 28 July 2015). Your answer will depend on future announcements.

Reliability of sources (page 118)

Q2: Both these predictions cover a wide range of outcomes, highlighting the difficulties in making an accurate estimate. Oil and Gas UK is an industry body so should be well-informed. The DECC is a government body, and although government statistics seemed sacrosanct a couple of decades ago, there can now be legitimate concern that they are politically tainted when not dealing with outright fact. A projection of future oil production gives a lot of scope for slanting in the preferred direction.

Quarterly output in the oil and gas sector (page 119)

Q3: The article you find should be checked for a recent date.

Brent Crude (page 120)

Q4: This varies and an up-to-date figure will be on the BBC website and many trading websites.

Market factors (page 121)

Q5:

Supply	Demand
Libya described as a "failed state"	Cold winter in the northern hemisphere
Soaring shale oil production in USA	Increasing miles per gallon of modern cars
	Reduced economic growth in China

North Sea job loss announcements (page 122)

Q6: There have been many such announcements in late 2014 and during 2015.

Q7: Each job loss reduces the spending power of an individual and their family, creating a negative multiplier in the communities in which they live. This will probably impact disproportionately on North East Scotland affecting local shopkeepers, but many purchases originate from outside this community so the effect will dissipate.

A competing positive multiplier as less is spent filling petrol tanks (and spent on more goods and services instead) may result in an outcome that is positive for the UK economy as a whole. Both effects may well be swamped (concealed) by other variables in the economic environment.

End of Topic 3 test (page 123)

Q8: b) between $100 and $120.

Q9: d) over 90%.

Q10: c) economic growth around the world.

Q11: a) new technology for developing shale oil.

Q12: d) all of the above

Topic 4: Global economic issues: globalisation

Globalisation definition (page 127)

Q1: The four basic aspects of globalisation identified by the IMF were:

- trade and transactions;
- capital and investment movements;
- migration and movement of people;
- the dissemination of knowledge.

Tata group (page 128)

Q2: The Tata group are an Indian multinational, conglomerate headquartered in Mumbai, India. They operate in the following business sectors: communications and information technology, engineering, materials, services, energy, consumer products, chemicals and core sciences. The Tata group have operations in more than 100 countries across six continents.

Major Tata companies include Tata Steel, Tata Motors, Tata Consultancy Services, Tata Power, Tata Chemicals, Tata Global Beverages, Tata Teleservices, Titan Industries, Tata Communications and Indian Hotels. Market capitalisation of all the 30 listed Tata companies is around $134 billion (as of March 2015). Approximately 70% of Tata revenue comes from outside India (figures from 2014-15).

Benefits of globalisation - video (page 129)

Q3: Norberg outlines the experience of Taiwan from the 1960s.

Taiwan adopted a deregulated market economy. Peasant farmers were given property rights and the ownership of land.

To begin with its selling points were low wages and long hours. It became well-known for producing low-technology plastic toys.

Working conditions in factories were poor by western standards, but economic growth and standards of living improved rapidly. The workers became more prosperous than they could have in the agricultural economy.

Foreign investment was attracted. There was investment in education. Skills, productivity and wages increased. Taiwan now has a technologically advanced economy. It was stated that Taiwan is 20 times richer than Kenya, a nation that was comparable just 50 years earlier.

Norberg expands his argument using the more recent example of Vietnam. He offers evidence that multinationals such as Nike have contributed to rising standards of living, and that far from damaging local enterprise, they have created a multiplier effect that extends into the wider community. A local entrepreneur is shown learning best practice from his multinational neighbour. Pay rates at Nike are much better than the local average income and, while Nike may eventually move on, they will have contributed to long-term benefits and economic advances.

By contrast, Kenya has not freed up its markets and given private enterprise its head. Land is owned by government, and regulations and costly trading licenses have restrained entrepreneurship. They are further handicapped by the international tariffs that globalisation seeks to reduce.

Benefits of globalisation (page 130)

Q4: Benefits of globalisation:

1. Improvements in standards of ***living***
2. Improvements in ***life*** expectancy
3. Improvements in ***literacy*** rates
4. Dramatic reductions in ***costs of production***
5. The spread of new ***technology***
6. Improved ***environmental*** performance
7. Improvements in working ***conditions***
8. Greater knowledge of and respect for other ***cultures***
9. Extension of ***democracy***
10. Increased ***international*** cooperation

Life expectancy (page 130)

Q5: The following figures are from Spring 2015:

a) UK 80, Japan 84, Canada 82;
b) Singapore 84, Taiwan 80, Brazil 73;
c) Vietnam 73;
d) Kenya 64.

As these figures are regularly updated, your answers may vary.

Note that you may not be entirely satisfied with the examples selected. Life expectancies have been affected unevenly by the spread of disease, e.g. HIV infection, and this can make the figures difficult to analyse and may cause doubts about the significance of globalisation in increasing life expectancy. It is also the case that the spread of disease is sometimes put down as a disadvantage of globalisation.

Consider carrying out your own further research into life expectancy and related figures such as infant mortality in countries at different stages of economic development and form your own considered conclusions.

Literacy rates (page 131)

Q6: The following figures are from Spring 2015:

a) Singapore 97%, Taiwan 98%, Brazil 93%;
b) Vietnam 94%;
c) Kenya 78%.

As these figures are regularly updated, your answers may vary.

Note that advanced economies such as the UK, Japan and Canada have literacy rates of 99% plus.

Effect of globalisation on the Taiwan, Brazil and Singapore economies (page 131)

Q7: There is no one solution, but any findings, for example on the CIA World Factbook (http://1.usa.gov/1FY6ErF) , on levels of economic growth, improvements in life expectancy, literacy rates, etc. are relevant.

Globalisation advantages and disadvantages (page 133)

Q8:

Advantages	Disadvantages
Dramatic reductions in costs of production	Destruction of traditional agricultural communities
Extension of democracy	Easier spread of disease
Greater knowledge of and respect for other cultures	Environmental damage
Improved environmental performance	Exploitation of workers
Improvements in life expectancy	Movement of skilled workers to richest countries
Improvements in literacy rates	Problems associated with the restructuring of economies
Improvements in standards of living	Recessions may become global
Improvements in working conditions	Unskilled workers in advanced economies face competition
Increased international cooperation	Use of child labour
The spread of new technology	Widening gap between richest and poorest countries

China's economy (page 134)

Q9: Low wages for manufacturing

Q10: In 2014 economic growth was 7%. This would exceed population growth lead to a rise in real incomes per head.

India's economy (page 134)

Q11: Your answer should look at:

- economic growth rates and standards of living;
- the changing pattern of employment (the percentages employed in primary/secondary/tertiary sectors over time);
- examples of the presence of multinational companies;
- the expansion of Indian based multinationals such as Tata;
- the changes in the Indian economy over the last few decades.

End of Topic 4 test (page 136)

Q12: c) a reduction in global warming.

Q13: b) labour mobility.

Q14: d) all of the above.

Q15: Among the responses you may include:

- evidence of manufacturing and call centre jobs being outsourced by UK companies;
- the presence of new brands on UK high streets and supermarkets;
- the extent that the migration of workers in and out of the UK has increased;
- the effect on the UK labour market and wages of the free movement of labour in the EU;
- an analysis of the causes of the UK's low inflation during the economic expansion between 1992 and 2007;
- examples of investment by foreign multinationals in the UK and examples of companies leaving the UK;
- the deregulation of the City of London in the "Big Bang" and the growth of London as an international financial centre;
- the impact on major parts of the Scottish economy (e.g. financial sector, whisky industry, seasonal agricultural employment).

Topic 5: Global economic issues: the European Union

Expansion of the EU (page 139)

Expected answer

Q1: Belgium, France, Italy, Luxembourg, Netherlands, West Germany, Ireland, Portugal, Spain, Austria and Finland.

Q2: Greece (2001), Slovenia (2007), Cyprus, Malta (both 2008), Slovakia (2009), Estonia (2011), Latvia (2014) and Lithuania (2015).

Single currency options (page 141)

Q3: A suitable article for research would be the following article on the Best Thinking website - htt p://bit.ly/1GIMWxc

Q4: I found several useful articles on the subject, for example:

- New Statesman website (http://bit.ly/1RjDNpp)
- Fortune website (http://for.tn/1MykDsk)

Advantages and disadvantages of joining the eurozone (page 143)

Q5:

Advantages	Disadvantages
Easier for consumers to compare prices in different countries	Devaluation of national currency no longer possible
Exchange rate certainty for firms within eurozone	Fiscal policy subject to strict rules that limit ability to borrow in recession
Multinational investment more likely	One interest rate set for all of eurozone
No commission on changing currency	Unexpected events may lead to eurozone economies diverging

EU enlargement (page 145)

Q6: For the UK the process of enlargement has several benefits. Consumers will have a greater ***choice*** of products. This increases ***competition*** which drives down ***prices***, leads to innovative behaviour by firms, and can improve the ***quality*** of products. Enlargement allows labour shortages to be met with ***foreign workers*** and keeps down wage inflation. It provides opportunities for UK based firms to improve ***profitability*** by moving to the lower wage economies of the new members.

Enlargement can create problems. UK workers will face more competition in the labour market and their ***wages*** are less likely to rise. Regional aid and CAP ***subsidies*** for the economic development of the new members may be expensive. Firms may move ***manufacturing*** and some service jobs to the new member countries to take advantage of lower wages and this will lead to some ***job losses*** in the UK.

Turkey - EU membership (page 147)

Q7: Benefits include that:

- it is a populous nation, that with a market economy and globalisation, has the potential to be a significant economic power;
- it provides links to energy sources to the East;
- for existing EU members, it greatly expands the single market and embraces globalisation;
- politically, the EU acting as one, would be an even more powerful block;
- culturally and politically, it provides a bridge to the Muslim world;
- it would provide a wider variety of goods for EU consumers, and be an alternative location for EU businesses to grow in.

Q8: Further progress is required on:

- women's rights;
- anti-corruption measures;
- judicial reform;
- agricultural reform;
- freedom of expression and the rights of minority religious groups.

Turkey also does not recognise Cyprus and this means it cannot open its ports and airports to all EU member states.

Turkey's current economic performance (page 147)

Q9: The solution to this would need regular updating, but you can expect to find wide disparities in areas such as GDP per capita for some time to come.

End of topic 5 test (page 149)

Q10: c) Croatia

Q11: d) 28

Q12: a) Italy

Q13: c) Romania and Bulgaria

Q14: b) Common Agricultural Policy

Q15: d) the widening of the EU by allowing in new member nations.

Q16: b) Portugal

Q17: b) the death penalty still exists in Turkey, and c) further progress is required on women's rights.

Q18: c) easily compare UK prices with those of other eurozone nations.

Topic 6: Economic growth in developing and emerging economies

World factbook - emerging economies (page 152)

Q1: No solution is available as GDP per capita and list of emerging economies will change over time.

World factbook - developing economies (page 153)

Q2: No solution is available as GDP per capita and list of developing economies will change over time.

Factors that delay economic growth (page 154)

Q3:

Land	Labour	Capital	Enterprise
low rainfall	poor health	inadequate roads	bureaucratic "red tape"
few natural resources	limited skills	little savings	few business skills

Economic growth of developing and emerging economies (page 155)

Q4: The figures will change every year so there is no definitive answer.

Economic growth of developing and emerging economies (page 155)

Q5: Education, sanitation and political stability

Q6: Any three of the following:

- high levels of private investment in business - much of it from foreign multinationals;
- high levels of investment by government in major infrastructure projects such as improvements to transport links;
- an economy rapidly diversifying into manufacturing;
- moves towards free trade and internationally open markets;
- the encouragement of entrepreneurship and a preference for free market solutions over state intervention;
- relaxed labour laws (workers are poorly protected from exploitation) and very competitive hourly wage rates.

Zambia's problems (page 157)

Q7: Zambia's problems include:

- dependency on the world market price of copper;
- Zambia is landlocked;
- resources have been mismanaged;
- corruption, associated with one-party rule until the 1990s;
- a high level of debt;
- disease (e.g. Malaria and Aids/HIV) - the adult prevalence rate of Aids/HIV is estimated at 15%;
- hosting refugees from civil wars in neighbouring Congo and Angola;
- failure to diversify the economy which is unattractive to foreign investment;
- poverty - millions of Zambians earn less than a dollar a day;
- air pollution and acid rain in the copper/cobalt mining/refining area;
- chemical pollution of water sources;
- lack of adequate water treatment;
- poaching of animal population;
- deforestation and resulting soil erosion.

Highly Indebted Poor Country (HIPC) Initiative (page 157)

Q8: To qualify, countries must have a level of debt that they cannot manage and must put into place structural reforms to their economy suggested by the IMF. It would be worthwhile reading some of the detailed information available on the web, for example at the IMF website (http://www.imf.org).

It provides debt relief and low interest loans to cancel or reduce external debt repayments to sustainable levels, meaning they can repay debts in a timely fashion in the future.

The price of copper (page 157)

Q9: I located the five year spot price of copper at the Kitko website (http://www.kitco.com/).

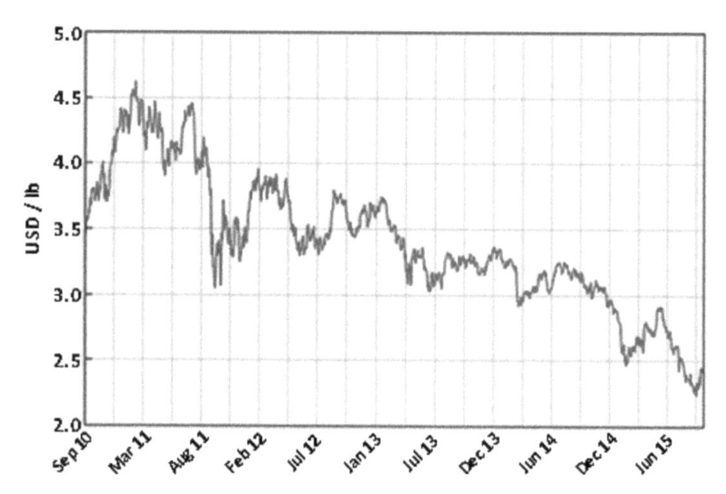

The price of copper has largely been in decline over the 5 years to 2015. Zambia is keen to diversify.

Another developing economy (page 157)

Q10: The solution will depend on your choice of country, so it is not possible to give a definitive solution.

The effect of rising oil prices on developing countries (page 159)

Q11: For your solution, extract the key points in the section above and add some research of your own. Make sure you acknowledge that some of the world's poorest countries actually have oil, and if they could manage this wealth in a wiser and less corrupt manner they make substantial improvements to education, infrastructure and living standards. For the majority of poor countries, rising oil prices will further strain their economies.

End of Topic 6 test (page 160)

Q12:

Brazil	Chad	***China***	***India***	Ireland
Italy	Malawi	Mali	***Nigeria***	***Russia***

Q13: b) levels of literacy and numeracy

Q14: c) sanitation

Q15: a) primary

Q16: The characteristics of emerging economies include:

- high levels of private investment in business - much of it from foreign multinationals;
- high levels of investment by government in major infrastructure projects such as improvements to transport links;
- an economy rapidly diversifying into manufacturing;
- moves towards free trade and internationally open markets;
- the encouragement of entrepreneurship and a preference for free market solutions over state intervention;
- relaxed labour laws (workers are poorly protected from exploitation) and very competitive hourly wage rates.

Topic 7: National and global economic issues test

National and global economic issues test (page 162)

Q1: c) long-term investment in infrastructure by government.

Q2: c) economic growth around the world.

Q3: d) all of the above

Q4: b) labour mobility.

Q5: d) all of the above.

Q6: d) they cannot match German levels of productivity.

Q7: c) set its own interest rates independently.

Q8: a) I) and II) only

Q9: d) I), II) and III)

Q10: b) Malawi, Brazil, Canada

Q11: Cuts in tax credits reduce the incomes of low wage earners. They have a high marginal propensity to consume. Without this income, they will reduce their level of consumption. This would lead to lower spending in shops and hence to lower orders to firms and unemployment. Economic growth would slow, VAT receipts would be less, and spending on unemployment benefits could increase. This would delay the achievement of a balanced budget. Cuts affecting those with the highest marginal propensity to consume could be counter-productive.

Cuts and delays in spending on infrastructure projects, and the holding down of public sector pay, could both also work through reduced economic growth to delay the achievement of a balanced budget.

Q12: A balanced budget stops interest rates on government borrowing soaring as the debt becomes unsustainable and there is a risk of default (as in Greece). It may prevent future tax rises or even result in lower tax rates.

The reduction of taxes and the public sector may be considered an encouragement to private enterprise. This has particular appeal to those who consider the private sector driven by the profit motive to be more efficient than public provision.

Answers to questions and activities for Researching an economic issue

Topic 1: How to organise your project

Project plan (page 169)

Q1: Possible solution:

- Topic selection: ***August***
- Research: ***September/October***
- Structure and first draft: ***November/December***
- Evaluation and redraft: ***January/February***
- Conclusion and final copy: ***March***
- Check/record all references: ***March***

Selecting a topic (page 171)

Q2: The following are good topics because they are both current and take the form of a question to be researched:

- Should the budget deficit be reduced?
- Is the UK headed for another recession?
- What should be the favoured currency option if Scotland gained independence?

End of Topic 1 test (page 173)

Q3: a) 7.5%

Q4: c) 4,000

Q5: c) 33.3%

Q6: a) current and economically significant.

Topic 2: How to research and write your project

Qualitative or quantitative research? (page 176)

Q1: **Quantitative research** is suited to expressing your findings numerically, e.g. in the form of tables and graphs. To gather information for this type of analysis, questions normally have a permitted range of answers from which the data is collated.

Qualitative research tends to provide varying responses that can offer more detail and subtle insight but are difficult to quantify. Open-ended responses and individual opinions have to be assessed and summarised.

Researchers are prone to placing more emphasis on quantitative data. Perhaps they feel confident with numbers, and the graphs look impressive and give weight to their conclusions? Do not underestimate the insight offered by the comments received through qualitative research - even though you may not get a pretty graph at the end!

A successful questionnaire (page 176)

Q2: The design of effective questionnaires is very difficult. You may be surprised by the work required to prepare a good questionnaire and collate the responses. As a result, the first principle is to keep it short and to the point.

There are many other noteworthy points which your research may advise on. For example, if respondents have to tick boxes use four options, not three or five. This will make it more difficult for the respondents to sit on the fence and cluster in the middle.

Project introduction (page 178)

Q3: The economic issue is clearly identified in the first few words. It is reasonable to claim the debate on the future of the Barnett Formula as a topical economic issue. Some clarification of the significance to the wider economy has been made.

Q4: The aims of the project are not clearly stated, and further development is required. Can the title been stated as an economic question to be investigated? It is too short to fulfill all the requirements of a good introduction

Project analysis and evaluation (page 179)

Q5: It offers a very basic beginning. We have some relevant facts (and providing they match stated aims for this project) they provide an opportunity for further development and analysis with examples and figures. For example, it begins to answer how Barnett operates; and whether Scotland is a net gainer overall on public spending per head (if these were aims). It also infers that there may be less need for it in the future, but much more detail is needed before conclusions can be reasonably drawn.

Q6: As an excerpt we cannot be too critical since we know not what the rest of the analysis showed. However this section:

a) is merely descriptive, making assertions which are not properly backed up;
b) is entirely devoid of figures. Are there no numbers (and graphs) that could be used to back up the assertions made?
c) misses an opportunity for an example such as the way in which "Barnett consequentials" for health spending in England have been used in Scotland;
d) deals with several issues quickly and should be divided into subsections for development.

Project conclusion (page 180)

Q7: This conclusion is summative.

If an aim were to consider what might replace the Barnett Formula, then this is a relevant conclusion. It could be backed up by having rates of unemployment across the UK regions (easily available) in the earlier analysis and perhaps quoting the unemployment rates in Scotland and North-East England in the conclusion.

Q8: Confirm that the conclusion:

a) matches up with a stated aim of this project;
b) derives from earlier findings and analysis;
c) is summative and does not just repeat earlier detailed analysis.

Project structure and coherence (page 181)

Q9: The front cover should indicate the word ***count***.

Q10: After redrafting you will need to review the page ***numbering*** on the contents page.

Q11: Your introduction should clearly justify your topic as both current and ***economic***.

Q12: Divide up the project with headings and ***subheadings***.

Q13: Your research will lead you directly to your ***conclusions***.

Q14: Note down your sources in a ***bibliography***.

Q15: Alongside relevant text place ***diagrams***.

Q16: The maximum number of appendices is ***three***.

Bibliography (page 183)

Q17: d) Verification

Q18: a) Bibliography

Q19: c) Referencing

Q20: b) Plagiarism

End of Topic 2 test (page 185)

Q21: a) A front cover

Q22: c) Arial, 12

Q23: a) producing a questionnaire.

Q24: b) double.

Q25: ***Time*** management is important.

Q26: Research widely and maintain a ***bibliography***.

Q27: Make sure the information is ***up-to-date***.

Q28: Start with a front cover that includes your name, the title, and the ***word count***.

Q29: Place ***diagrams*** alongside relevant text.

Q30: Draw your ***conclusions*** from the evidence.

Topic 3: Researching an economic issue test

Researching an economic issue test (page 188)

Q1: (a) good time management and (b) wide research that you record.

Q2: (b) must be on a topical economic issue and (c) should not exceed 4,000 words.

Q3: (b) follow logically from your findings and analysis, (c) match up with the aims set out at the start of the project and (d) avoid the detailed repetition of material presented earlier in the project.

Q4: (c) Adding a graphic to the front cover

Q5: (a) interviewing individuals for your research and recording what they say.

Q6: (a) assessing the source for reliability and possible bias and (c) the application of economic theory to the data.

Q7: (a) missing opportunities to provide relevant graphs and tables and (c) producing a project that is merely descriptive.

Q8: (b) Has inequality in the UK increased in recent years?

BV - #0012 - 270420 - C0 - 210/148/14 - PB - 9781911057703